# MY FIRST
# ENGLISH-FRENCH
# DICTIONARY

*Mon premier dictionnaire anglais-fra...*

*English text :* ELLEN WALES WALPOLE
*French text :* ANNE LEBOUCHER
*Pronunciation and Grammar :* HUGH SHELLEY
*Pictures :* GERTRUDE ELLIOTT

Prepared under the supervision of
RENÉ GUILLOT
Professor at the Lycée Condorcet, Paris

*A SIMPLE INTRODUCTION TO GRAMMAR APPEARS ON PAGES 4-7
AND A GUIDE TO PRONUNCIATION ON PAGE 98*

First Published 1962
Seventh Impression 1972
Published by THE HAMLYN PUBLISHING GROUP LIMITED
London • New York • Sydney • Toronto
Hamlyn House, Feltham, Middlesex, England
© 1961, 1962 by Western Publishing Company Inc.
ISBN 0 601 07200 6
Printed in Czechoslovakia by Svoboda, Prague
51031/7

# A FIRST FRENCH GRAMMAR

## How to make a sentence

In any language, a sentence is a group of words that makes a statement.

> EXAMPLE: **Paul lit le journal.**
>
> Paul reads the newspaper.

But an English sentence is not always translated word for word into French.

> EXAMPLE: A chief is a leader.
>
> **Un chef est celui qui dirige.**
>
> (A chief is he who directs.)

---

## The noun

A noun is the name of a person, place or thing. In English, only persons and animals are "he" or "she". **Paul** is a "he". But in French *every* noun is either a "he" or a "she". These are called genders; a "he" noun is masculine, a "she" noun is feminine. **Balloon** in French is masculine: **le ballon**. **House** in French is feminine: **la maison**.

---

## The adjective

An adjective is a word that says what a noun is like. In French, if the noun is masculine, the adjective must be masculine too, and if the noun is feminine, the adjective must be feminine. A feminine adjective almost always adds E to the masculine form.

> EXAMPLE: **Le grand loup**      The big wolf
>
> **La grande fleur**      The big flower

Most French adjectives, however, follow their noun.

> EXAMPLE: **Le chat noir**      The black cat
>
> **La fille heureuse**      The happy girl

# The article

An article is a little word in front of a noun. In English the articles are **the** and **a** or **an**. In French, they are **le** (masculine) or **la** (feminine) and **un** (masculine) or **une** (feminine).

EXAMPLE:  **le calendrier**   the calendar   **un couteau**   a knife
             **la ficelle**      the string     **une cage**    a cage

When a noun, however, is used in a general sense, the article **a** (or **an**) in English is translated by **le** or **la** in French.

EXAMPLE:  **Le bras est une partie du corps.**  **La pomme est un fruit.**
           An arm is a part of the body.     An apple is a fruit.

Names of persons do not have articles.

      EXAMPLE:  **Paul a un chien**.     Paul has a dog.

---

# The plural

When there is more than one of anything, we say that it is in the plural. In French, if the noun is in the plural, the article must be in the plural too. **Les** is the plural of **le** and **la**. **Des** is the plural of **un** and **une**. As in English, French nouns in the plural almost always add S at the end of the word.

EXAMPLE:

| | | | |
|---|---|---|---|
| **le canard** | the duck | **les canards** | the ducks |
| **la poule** | the hen | **les poules** | the hens |
| **un jardin** | a garden | **des jardins** | gardens |
| **une chaise** | a chair | **des chaises** | chairs |

Plural adjectives also add S but keep the gender of the noun

      EXAMPLE:  **les crayons bleus**     the blue pencils
                    **les jolies poupées**     the pretty dolls

---

# The pronoun

A pronoun is a word we use in place of a noun. Instead of saying **Paul has a spade,** we can say: **He has a spade.** It is the same in French: **Il a une bêche.** The pronouns are:

| | | | |
|---|---|---|---|
| **Je** | I | **Nous** | We |
| **Tu** | You | **Vous** | You |
| **Il** | He, It | **Ils** | They |
| **Elle** | She, It | **Elles** | They |

**Tu** is only used when speaking to the family or close friends.

**It** which is neuter in English is translated in French by either **il** or **elle** according to the gender of the noun to which it refers.

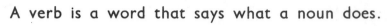

# The verb

A verb is a word that says what a noun does.

> EXAMPLE: **Paul aime le chien.**   Paul likes the dog.
> **Le chien joue.**   The dog plays.

**Likes (aime)** and **plays (joue)** are verbs.

These verbs are shown in the "present". The present describes what **is** happening.  Now let's learn a verb with all the pronouns.

| | | | |
|---|---|---|---|
| **Je joue** | I play | **Nous jouons** | We play |
| **Tu joues** | You play | **Vous jouez** | You play |
| **Il** / **Elle** } **joue** | He / She } plays | **Ils** / **Elles** } **jouent** | They play |

Two most important verbs to learn are: **être** (to be) and **avoir** (to have).

| | | | |
|---|---|---|---|
| **Je suis** | I am | **J'ai** | I have |
| **Tu es** | You are | **Tu as** | You have |
| **Il** / **Elle** } **est** | He, It / She, It } is | **Il** / **Elle** } **a** | He, It / She, It } has |
| **Nous sommes** | We are | **Nous avons** | We have |
| **Vous êtes** | You are | **Vous avez** | You have |
| **Ils** / **Elles** } **sont** | They are | **Ils** / **Elles** } **ont** | They have |

EXAMPLE:

| | |
|---|---|
| **Qui a un grand chien?** | Who has a big dog? |
| **J'ai un grand chien.** | I have a big dog. |
| **Nous jouons avec la balle.** | We play with the ball. |
| **Elle est bleue.** | It is blue. |
| **Suzanne est ma sœur.** | Suzanne is my sister. |
| **Suzanne, aimes-tu jouer?** | Suzanne, do you like to play? |

A verb may also be in the "past".  The past describes what **has** happened. With most verbs it is made with the present tense of **avoir** (to have).

| | |
|---|---|
| **J'ai joué** | I played |
| **Tu as joué** | You played |
| **Il** / **Elle** } **a joué** | He / She } played |
| **Nous avons joué** | We played |
| **Vous avez joué** | You played |
| **Ils** / **Elles** } **ont joué** | They played |

| | | | |
|---|---|---|---|
| J'ai été | I have been | J'ai eu | I have had |
| Tu as été | You have been | Tu as eu | You have had |
| Il / Elle } a été | He, It / She, It } has been | Il / Elle } a eu | He, It / She, It } has had |
| Nous avons été | We have been | Nous avons eu | We have had |
| Vous avez été | You have been | Vous avez eu | You have had |
| Ils / Elles } ont été | They have been | Ils / Elles } ont eu | They have had |

The few verbs which make their past with the present of **être** are mostly verbs of motion.

EXAMPLE:

| | | | |
|---|---|---|---|
| Je suis allé | I went | Nous sommes arrivés | We arrived |
| Tu es venu | You came | Vous êtes entrés | You came in |
| Il est monté | He climbed | Ils sont partis | They left |

Thirdly, a verb may be used in the "future". The future describes what **will** happen. Let us learn the future of our three verbs.

| | |
|---|---|
| Je jouerai | I shall play |
| Tu joueras | You will play |
| Il / Elle } jouera | He / She } will play |
| Nous jouerons | We shall play |
| Vous jouerez | You will play |
| Ils / Elles } joueront | They will play |

| | |
|---|---|
| Je serai | I shall be |
| Tu seras | You will be |
| Il / Elle } sera | He, It / She, It } will be |
| Nous serons | We shall be |
| Vous serez | You will be |
| Ils / Elles } seront | They will be |

| | |
|---|---|
| J'aurai | I shall have |
| Tu auras | You will have |
| Il / Elle } aura | He, It / She, It } will have |
| Nous aurons | We shall have |
| Vous aurez | You will have |
| Ils / Elles } auront | They will have |

to eat
*manger*

to read
*lire*

to walk
*marcher*

to push
*pousser*

to jump
*sauter*

to skip
*sauter à la corde*

to sleep
*dormir*

to climb
*grimper*

to hop
*sauter à cloche-pied*

to run
*courir*

to sing
*chanter*

to wash
*se laver*

to write
*écrire*

to skate
*patiner*

to kick
*frapper*

to pull
*tirer*

to dig
*creuser*

to build
*construire*

to dance
*danser*

to drink  *boire*

to paint
*peindre*

to sew
*coudre*

to slide
*glisser*

to swim  *nager*

to dress
*s'habiller*

These are **acts**.
*Ce sont des **actions**.*

8

# A a

First letter of the alphabet.
*Première lettre de l'alphabet.*

## a, an    un, une

Here are **a** lemon and **an** apple.
*Voici **un** citron et **une** pomme.*

## to be able    pouvoir

Ann **is** not **able** to touch her toes.
*Anne ne **peut** pas toucher ses orteils.*

John **is able** to touch his toes.
*Jean **peut** toucher ses orteils.*

| I am able | I shall be able | I was able |
|---|---|---|
| Je peux | Je pourrai | J'ai pu |

## about
### au sujet de, environ

1. I shall tell you a story **about** an umbrella on a beach.
   *Je vous raconterai une histoire **au sujet d'**un parasol sur une plage.*

2. It is **about** time to go to bed.
   *Il est **environ** l'heure de se coucher.*

## above    au dessus de

The plane is **above** the clouds.
*L'avion est **au-dessus des** nuages.*

## across    en travers de

The pen is **across** the pencil.
*Le porte-plume est **en travers du** crayon.*

## to act    jouer

The players **act** on the stage.
*Les acteurs **jouent** sur la scène.*

| I act | I shall act | I acted |
|---|---|---|
| Je joue | Je jouerai | J'ai joué |

## to add
### ajouter, additionner

1. Mother **added** two apples to three apples.
   *Maman **a ajouté** deux pommes à trois pommes.*

2. **Add** two apples and three apples and you will have five.
   ***Additionnez** deux pommes et trois pommes et vous en aurez cinq.*

| I add | I shall add | I added |
|---|---|---|
| J'additionne | J'additionnerai | J'ai additionné |
| J'ajoute | J'ajouterai | J'ai ajouté |

## to be afraid
### avoir peur

The cat **is afraid** to jump.
*Le chat **a peur** de sauter.*

| I am afraid | I shall be afraid | I have been afraid |
|---|---|---|
| J'ai peur | J'aurai peur | J'ai eu peur |

## after    après

1. The dog ran **after** the cat.
   *Le chien courait **après** le chat.*

2. **After** school we run and play.
   ***Après** l'école nous courons et nous jouons.*

## again    encore

If at first you do not succeed, try, try **again**.
*Si vous ne réussissez pas la première fois, essayez, essayez **encore**.*

## against    contre

1. Bob is leaning **against** the tree.
   *Bob s'appuie **contre** l'arbre.*

2. The goats are fighting **against** each other.
   *Les chèvres se battent l'une **contre** l'autre.*

## age    âge

Grandfather is fifty-three years old.
*Grand-père a cinquante trois ans.*

Baby is four months old.
*Bébé a quatre mois.*

They are not the same **age**.
*Ils ne sont pas du même **âge**.*

## to agree  être d'accord

I think cats are nice.
*Je pense que les chats sont gentils.*

You think cats are bad.
*Tu penses que les chats sont méchants.*

We do not **agree** about cats.
*Nous ne **sommes** pas **d'accord** au sujet des chats.*

| I agree | I shall agree | I agreed |
|---|---|---|
| *Je suis d'accord* | *Je serai d'accord* | *J'ai été d'accord* |

## air  air

There is a covering of **air** around the earth.
*Il y a une couche d'**air** autour de la terre.*

We breathe **air**.
*Nous respirons l'**air**.*

Birds fly in the **air**.
*Les oiseaux volent dans l'**air**.*

## aircraft  avion

An **aircraft** can fly far.
*Un **avion** peut voler loin.*

## all  tout

Henry drank **all** his milk.
*Henri a bu **tout** son lait.*

Baby did not drink **all** his milk.
*Bébé n'a pas bu **tout** son lait.*

## almost
*presque, à peu près*

1. John **almost** caught a fish.
   *Jean a **presque** attrapé un poisson.*

2. It is **almost** noon.
   *Il est **à peu près** midi.*

## alone  seul

The little bear is **alone** on the shelf.
*Le petit ours est **seul** sur l'étagère.*

He went outdoors **alone**.
*Il est sorti **seul**.*

## alphabet  alphabet

There are 26 letters in our **alphabet**.
*Il y a 26 lettres dans notre **alphabet**.*

They are ABCDEFGHIJKLMNOPQRSTUVWXYZ.
*Ce sont ABCDEFGHIJKLMNOPQRSTUVWXYZ.*

## already  déjà

Have you read the book **already** ?
*Avez-vous **déjà** lu le livre ?*

## also  aussi

You may have a red balloon, **also**.
*Vous pouvez **aussi** avoir un ballon rouge.*

## always  toujours

They **always** take their lunch to school.
*Ils emportent **toujours** leur déjeuner à l'école.*

I **always** wear a belt.
*Je porte **toujours** une ceinture.*

## among
*entre, au milieu de, parmi*

1. We divided the ice cream **among** the children.
   *Nous avons partagé la glace **entre** les enfants.*

2. The pigs are running **among** the chickens.
   *Les cochons courent **au milieu des** poulets.*

3. **Among** the trees on the square is an oak.
   *Parmi les arbres, sur la place, il y a un chêne.*

## and  et

Jane **and** Bill have a cat **and** a dog.
*Jeanne **et** Bill ont un chat **et** un chien.*

# animal    *animal*

**Animals** are living things that move about.
*Les **animaux** sont des êtres vivants qui bougent.*

In order that we may learn their French gender, the names are preceded by the article.
*Afin que nous puissions apprendre leur genre en français, les noms sont précédés de l'article.*

kitten
*le chaton*

cat
*le chat*

rat
*le rat*

dog
*le chien*

puppy
*le chiot*

sheep
*le mouton*

lamb
*l'agneau (le)*

chipmunk
*le tamia*

calf
*le veau*

cow
*la vache*

crocodile
*le crocodile*

rabbit
*le lapin*

horse
*le cheval*

pig
*le cochon*

butterfly
*le papillon*

tortoise
*la tortue*

deer
*le cerf*

beaver
*le castor*

skunk
*la moufette*

lion
*le lion*

fawn
*le faon*

giraffe
*la girafe*

tiger
*le tigre*

elephant
*l'éléphant (le)*

kangaroo
*le kangourou*

monkey
*le singe*

squirrel
*l'écureuil (le)*

camel
*le chameau*

bear
*l'ours (le)*

mouse
*la souris*

fox
*le renard*

frog
*la grenouille*

tadpole
*le têtard*

rhinoceros
*le rhinocéros*

flea
*la puce*

ostrich
*l'autruche (la)*

zebra
*le zèbre*

kid
*le chevreau*

goat
*la chèvre*

owl
*le hibou*

hippopotamus
*l'hippopotame (le)*

snake
*le serpent*

lizard
*le lézard*

fish
*le poisson*

These are **animals.**
*Ce sont des **animaux.***

11

## angry    fâché

Do not annoy the lion with your stick.
*N'agacez pas le lion avec votre bâton.*

He will get **angry**.
*Il sera **fâché**.*

## another    un autre

Here is a (Teddy) bear.
*Voici un ours.*
Here is **another** (Teddy) bear.
*Voici **un autre** ours.*

The boys and girls are playing with one **another**.
*Les garçons et les filles jouent les uns avec les **autres**.*

## answer    to answer
## réponse    répondre

The teacher asks a question.
*Le professeur pose une question.*

1. The children give the **answer**.
   *Les enfants donnent la **réponse**.*

2. They **answer** the teacher.
   *Ils **répondent** au professeur.*

| I answer | I shall answer | I answered |
|----------|----------------|------------|
| *Je réponds* | *Je répondrai* | *J'ai répondu* |

## any    quelques, aucun

Are there **any** biscuits left?
*Reste-t-il **quelques** biscuits?*

No, there are not **any**.
*Non, il n'y en a **aucun**.*

## anything    quelque chose

Is there **anything** in the cupboard ?
*Y a-t-il **quelque chose** dans l'armoire ?*

## apple    pomme

An **apple** is a fruit.
*La **pomme** est un fruit.*

## arm    bras

An **arm** is a part of the body.
*Le **bras** est une partie du corps.*

## army    armée

In the **army** soldiers use guns,
tanks and planes.

*Dans **l'armée** les soldats se servent
de canons, de chars et d'avions.*

## around    autour de

The children are running **around**
the tree.
*Les enfants courent **autour** de l'arbre.*

## as    aussi...que, comme

1. Tom ran **as** fast **as** he could.
   *Tom courait **aussi** vite **qu'**il pouvait.*

2. Betty went to the party, dressed **as** a fairy
   *Elisabeth est allée à la fête, habillée **comme** une fée.*

## to ask    demander

**Ask** your mother if you may come.
***Demandez** à votre mère si vous pouvez venir.*

I **asked** her. She said " Yes ".
*Je le lui ai **demandé**. Elle a dit " oui ".*

| I ask | I shall ask | I asked |
|-------|-------------|---------|
| *Je demande* | *Je demanderai* | *J'ai demandé* |

12

**asleep**  *endormi*

Jenny is **asleep**.
*Jeannette est **endormie**.*

**at**  *à, au*

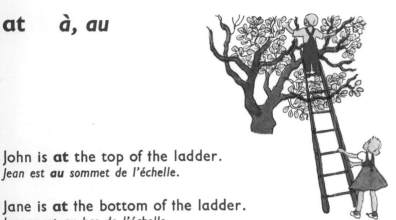

John is **at** the top of the ladder.
*Jean est **au** sommet de l'échelle.*

Jane is **at** the bottom of the ladder.
*Jeanne est **au** bas de l'échelle.*

**attract**  *attirer*

The light **attracts** the moth.
*La lumière **attire** le papillon de nuit.*

**awake**  *réveillé*

Bob is **awake**.
*Bob est **réveillé**.*

**axe**  *hache*

An **axe** is for chopping wood.
*La **hache** sert à couper le bois.*

---

# B b

Second letter of the alphabet.
*Seconde lettre de l'alphabet.*

**baboon**  *babouin*

A **baboon** is an animal.
*Le **babouin** est un animal.*

**baby**  *bébé*

Our **baby** is four weeks old.
*Notre **bébé** a quatre semaines.*

**back**  *dos*

Tim carries his books on his **back**.
*Tim porte ses livres sur son **dos**.*

**bad**  *mauvais, méchant*

1. This is a **bad** apple.
   *Voici une **mauvaise** pomme.*

2. These **bad** boys are stealing peaches.
   *Ces **méchants** garçons volent des pêches.*

**bag**  *sac*

| handbag | paper bag | bag of sand |
| --- | --- | --- |
| *sac à main* | *sac en papier* | *sac de sable* |

**Bags** are used for carrying things.
*Les **sacs** servent à transporter des objets.*

Ladies carry **handbags**.
*Les dames portent des **sacs à main**.*

## baggage  *bagage*

a suitcase
*une valise*

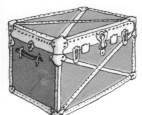

a trunk
*une malle*

Our **baggage** is full of things to take on our trip.
*Nos **bagages** sont pleins d'objets à emporter en voyage.*

## ball  *balle, pelote*

a rubber ball
*une balle de caoutchouc*

a ball of string
*une pelote de ficelle*

The **ball** is round.
*La **balle** est ronde.*

## balloon  *ballon*

The **balloon** floats in the air.
*Le **ballon** flotte dans l'air.*

## banana  *banane*

A **banana** is a yellow fruit.
*La **banane** est un fruit jaune.*

## band

### orchestre

### ruban

1. The **band** plays music in the park.
   *L'**orchestre** joue de la musique dans le parc.*

2. He has a **band** on his hat.
   *Il a un **ruban** à son chapeau.*

## bank  *rive*
### *banque*

1. Rivers have two **banks**.
   *Les fleuves ont deux **rives**.*

2. Father puts his money in the city **bank**.
   *Papa dépose son argent à la **banque** de la ville.*

## barber  *coiffeur*

A **barber** cuts hair.
*Le **coiffeur** coupe les cheveux.*

## barn  *grange*

A **barn** is a building on a farm.
*La **grange** est un bâtiment de ferme.*

## barrel  *tonneau*

A **barrel** is round and made of wood.
*Le **tonneau** est rond et en bois.*

## basin  *lavabo*

I wash my hands in a **basin**.
*Je me lave les mains dans un **lavabo**.*

## basket  *panier*

shopping basket
*panier à provisions*

clothes basket
*panier à linge*

**Baskets** are made of wood or straw.
*Les **paniers** sont en bois ou en paille.*

## bat
### batte

Bruce has a **bat**.
*Bruce a une* **batte**.

He uses it to play cricket.
*Il s'en sert pour jouer au* **cricket**.

## bat   chauve-souris

A **bat** is an animal that flies at night.
*La* **chauve-souris** *est un animal qui vole la nuit.*

## bath   bain   baignoire

1. Taking a **bath** makes you clean.
   *Prendre un* **bain** *vous rend propre.*

2. We use the big **bath**.
   *Nous utilisons la grande* **baignoire**.

   The **bath** is in the **bath**room.
   *La* **baignoire** *est dans la salle de* **bain**.

## to be   être

1. I **am** French.
   *Je* **suis** *français.*

2. Patsy **is** a girl.
   *Patsy est une* **fille**.

3. John and Henry **are** the same age.
   *Jean et Henri* **sont** *du même âge.*

4. **Be** good.
   **Sois** *sage.*

5. We **will be** home at nine o'clock.
   *Nous* **serons** *rentrés à neuf heures.*

| I am | I shall be | I was |
|------|-----------|-------|
| Je suis | Je serai | J'ai été |

## bead   perle

**Beads** are strung on a string.
*Les* **perles** *sont enfilées sur un fil.*

## bean   haricot

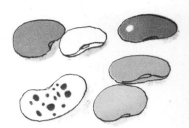

**Beans** are vegetables.
*Les* **haricots** *sont des légumes.*

**Beans** are good to eat.
*Les* **haricots** *sont bons à manger.*

## bear   ours

A **bear** is an animal with a thick fur coat.
*L'*ours *est un animal à fourrure épaisse.*

There are white **bears**, brown **bears** and black **bears**.
*Il y a des* **ours** *blancs, des* **ours** *bruns et des* **ours** *noirs.*

## beautiful   beau, belle   beaux, belles

The world is **beautiful**.
*Le monde est* **beau**.

Clouds are **beautiful**.
*Les nuages sont* **beaux**.

**Beautiful** music is pleasing to hear.
*La* **belle** *musique est agréable à entendre.*

We like **beautiful** things.
*Nous aimons les* **belles** *choses.*

## because
### parce que

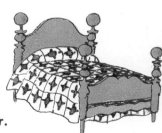

Paula's plant died **because** she did not water it.
*La plante de Paule est morte* **parce qu'**elle ne l'a pas arrosée.*

## bed   lit

We sleep in a **bed**.
*Nous dormons dans un* **lit**.

The **bed** is in the bedroom.
*Le* **lit** *est dans la chambre à coucher.*

## bee
## abeille

bumblebee
*bourdon*

honeybee
*.abeille ouvrière*

**Bees** provide us with honey.
*Les **abeilles** nous fournissent le miel.*

## before    *devant, avant*

1. Jack stands **before** Jane.
   *Jacques se tient **devant** Jeanne.*

2. We wash our hands **before** each meal.
   *Nous nous lavons les mains **avant** chaque repas.*

## to begin    *commencer*

We **begin** to write at the top of the page.
*Nous **commençons** à écrire en haut de la page.*

| I begin | I shall begin | I began |
|---|---|---|
| *Je commence* | *Je commencerai* | *J'ai commencé* |

## behind    *derrière*

Harold is **behind** the door.
*Harold est **derrière** la porte.*

## to believe    *croire*

Do you **believe** in fairies?
***Croyez**-vous aux fées?*

| I believe | I shall believe | I believed |
|---|---|---|
| *Je crois* | *Je croirai* | *J'ai cru* |

## bell
## cloche,
## sonnette

1. The school **bell** rings in the morning.
   *La **cloche** de l'école sonne le matin.*
   The church **bells** ring on Sunday.
   *Les **cloches** de l'église sonnent le dimanche.*
2. Mary rings the **doorbell**.
   *Marie fait marcher la **sonnette**.*

## to belong    *appartenir*

Does this **belong** to you?
*Ceci vous **appartient**-il?*

| I belong | I shall belong | I belonged |
|---|---|---|
| *J'appartiens* | *J'appartiendrai* | *J'ai appartenu* |

## below    *sous*

The little picture is **below** the big picture.
*Le petit tableau est **sous** le grand tableau.*

## belt    *ceinture*

A **belt** is a strip of leather or cloth.
*Une **ceinture** est une bande de cuir ou d'étoffe.*

A **belt** is worn around the waist.
*Une **ceinture** se porte autour de la taille.*

## to bend
## *plier, se pencher, courber*

1. This strong man **bent** the iron bar.
   *Cet homme fort **a plié** la barre de fer.*

2. John **bends** to pick up the ball.
   *Jean **se penche** pour ramasser la balle.*

3. Trees **bend** in the wind.
   *Les arbres **se courbent** dans le vent.*

| I bend | I shall bend | I bent |
|---|---|---|
| *Je plie* | *Je plierai* | *J'ai plié* |
| *Je me penche* | *Je me pencherai* | *Je me suis penché* |
| *Je courbe* | *Je courberai* | *J'ai courbé* |

## beside    *à côté de*

Paula sits **beside** John.
*Paule est assise **à côté de** Jean.*

16

## between    *entre*

Mary is **between** Tom and Bill.
*Marie est **entre** Tom et Bill.*

## Bible    *Bible*

The **Bible** contains the Old and New Testaments.
*La **Bible** comprend l'Ancien et le Nouveau Testaments.*

## bicycle    *bicyclette*

**Bicycles** have two wheels.
*Les **bicyclettes** ont deux roues.*

Walter is riding a **bicycle**.
*Walter monte à **bicyclette**.*

## big    *grand*

The store is **big**.
*Le magasin est **grand**.*

It is **bigger** than the house.
*Il est **plus grand** que la maison.*

The bank building is the **biggest** of the three.
*Le bâtiment de la banque est le **plus grand** des trois.*

## bird    *oiseau*

A **bird** is an animal with feathers.
*Un **oiseau** est un animal à plumes.*

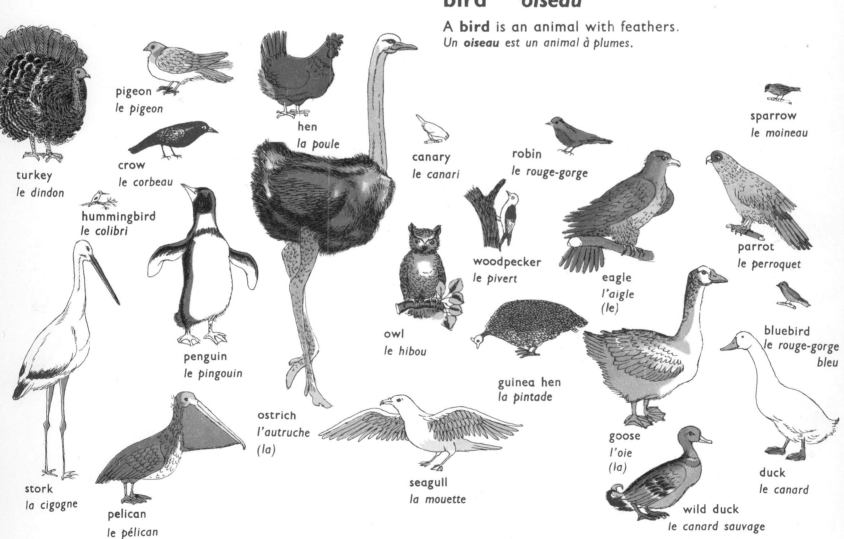

turkey
*le dindon*

pigeon
*le pigeon*

crow
*le corbeau*

hummingbird
*le colibri*

penguin
*le pingouin*

stork
*la cigogne*

pelican
*le pélican*

hen
*la poule*

ostrich
*l'autruche (la)*

owl
*le hibou*

canary
*le canari*

woodpecker
*le pivert*

seagull
*la mouette*

guinea hen
*la pintade*

robin
*le rouge-gorge*

eagle
*l'aigle (le)*

goose
*l'oie (la)*

wild duck
*le canard sauvage*

sparrow
*le moineau*

parrot
*le perroquet*

bluebird
*le rouge-gorge bleu*

duck
*le canard*

These are **birds**; they are shown here with their genders.
*Ce sont des **oiseaux**; ils sont ici désignés avec leurs genres.*

17

## to bite    *mordre*

Bruce **has bitten** the biscuit.
*Bruce **a mordu** dans le biscuit.*

| I bite | I shall bite | I bit |
|---|---|---|
| *Je mords* | *Je mordrai* | *J'ai mordu* |

## bitter    *amer*

**Bitter** things do not taste sweet.
*Les choses **amères** n'ont pas un goût sucré.*

## black    *noir*

**Black** is a colour.
*Le **noir** est une couleur.*

## blackboard
## *tableau noir*

The teacher writes on the **blackboard**.
*Le professeur écrit sur le **tableau noir**.*

## blade    *lame, brin*

1. We cut with the **blade** of a knife.
   *Nous coupons avec la **lame** du couteau.*

2. Here is a **blade** of grass.
   *Voici un **brin** d'herbe.*

## blind    *aveugle*

The **blind** cannot see.
*Les **aveugles** ne peuvent pas voir.*

## block    to block
## *cube*    *bloquer*

1. Jack is playing with his **blocks**.
   *Jacques joue avec ses **cubes**.*

2.

| It blocks | It will block | It blocked |
|---|---|---|
| *Il bloque* | *Il bloquera* | *Il a bloqué* |

## blue    *bleu*

**Blue** is a colour.
*Le **bleu** est une couleur.*

## board    *planche*

A **board** is a flat piece of wood.
*Une **planche** est un morceau de bois plat.*

## boat
## *bateau*

| rowboat | steamboat | sailing boat |
|---|---|---|
| *bateau à rames* | *bateau à vapeur* | *bateau à voiles* |

We crossed the lake in a **boat**.
*Nous avons traversé le lac en **bateau**.*

## body    *corps*

My **body** is covered with skin.
*Mon **corps** est recouvert de peau.*

The cat's **body** is covered with fur.
*Le **corps** du chat est recouvert de fourrure.*

## bone    *arête, os*

1. These are the **bones** of a fish.
   *Voici les **arêtes** d'un poisson.*

2. Bob gives Rover a **bone**.
   *Bob donne un **os** à Rover.*

   Can you feel the **bones** in your body?
   *Pouvez-vous sentir les **os** de votre corps?*

## bonnet    *bonnet*

The baby has a blue **bonnet**.
*Le bébé a un **bonnet** bleu.*

## book    *livre*

A **book** has many printed pages.
*Un **livre** a beaucoup de pages imprimées.*

This is a **book**.
*Ceci est un **livre**.*

## bottle    *bouteille*

milk bottle
*bouteille de lait*

**Bottles** are made of glass.
*Les bouteilles sont en verre.*

**Bottles** hold liquids.
*Les bouteilles contiennent des liquides.*

medicine bottle
*bouteille de médicament*

## bottom    *fond*

The stone fell to the **bottom** of the well.
*La pierre est tombée au fond du puits.*

## bow    *nœud, arc*

1. Sue has a pink **bow** in her hair.
   *Suzanne a un nœud rose dans les cheveux.*

2. Jack has a **bow** and arrow.
   *Jacques a un arc et une flèche.*

## bowl    *bol*

A **bowl** is a deep container.
*Un bol est un récipient profond.*

## box    *boîte*

We keep things in **boxes**.
*Nous gardons les objets dans des boîtes.*

## boy    *garçon*

Tom is a **boy**.
*Tom est un garçon.*

## branch    *branche*

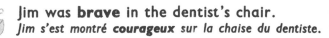

A **branch** fell off the tree.
*Une branche tomba de l'arbre.*

## brave    *courageux*

Jim was **brave** in the dentist's chair.
*Jim s'est montré courageux sur la chaise du dentiste.*

## bread    *pain*

**Bread** is made from flour.
*Le pain est fait avec de la farine.*

Here is a loaf of **bread**.
*Voici une miche de pain.*

## to break    *casser*

Did Ann **break** her doll ?
*Anne a-t-elle cassé sa poupée ?*

| I break | I shall break | I broke |
|---------|---------------|---------|
| *Je casse* | *Je casserai* | *J'ai cassé* |

## breakfast    *petit déjeuner*

**Breakfast** is the first meal of the day.
*Le petit déjeuner est le premier repas de la journée.*

## breath    *souffle*         to breathe    *respirer*

1. **Breathe** through your nose.
   *Respirez par le nez.*

2. There is not a **breath** of wind.
   *Il n'y a pas un souffle de vent.*

| I breathe | I shall breathe | I breathed |
|-----------|-----------------|------------|
| *Je respire* | *Je respirerai* | *J'ai respiré* |

# bridge
## pont

The **bridge** spans the river.
*Le **pont** enjambe la rivière.*

# bright
## brillant

How **bright** the sun is today!
*Que le soleil est **brillant** aujourd'hui!*

# broom    balai

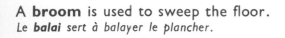

A **broom** is used to sweep the floor.
*Le **balai** sert à balayer le plancher.*

# brother    frère

Tom is my **brother**.
*Tom est mon **frère**.*

# brush
## brosse

 clothes brush
*brosse à habits*

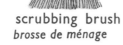 scrubbing brush
*brosse de ménage*

 paint brush
*pinceau*

tooth brush
*brosse à dents*

**Brushes** are used for cleaning or painting.
*Les **brosses** servent à nettoyer ou à peindre.*

# bud    bourgeon

The **bud** will open into a leaf or flower.
*Le **bourgeon** s'ouvrira pour devenir fleur ou feuille.*

# to build    construire

Julie helps Bruce to **build** a tower.
*Julie aide Bruce à **construire** une tour.*

| I build | I shall build | I built |
|---|---|---|
| *Je construis* | *Je construirai* | *J'ai construit* |

# building    bâtiment

Houses, churches and schools are **buildings**.
*Les maisons, les églises et les écoles sont des **bâtiments**.*

These are **buildings**.
*Voici des **bâtiments**.*

# bulb    bulbe, ampoule

1. This **bulb** will grow into a tulip.
   *Ce **bulbe** va devenir une tulipe.*
2. The electric light **bulb** lights the room at night.
   *L'**ampoule** électrique éclaire la chambre la nuit.*

   The light **bulb** is the same shape as the tulip **bulb**.
   *L'**ampoule** électrique a la même forme que le **bulbe** de la tulipe.*

# bun    brioche

Judy made some **buns**.
*Judith a fait des **brioches**.*

# burn    brûlure
# to burn    brûler

1. Joe has a **burn** on his wrist.
   *Joe a une **brûlure** au poignet.*
2. Wood **burns**.
   *Le bois **brûle**.*

| I burn | I shall burn | I burned |
|---|---|---|
| *Je brûle* | *Je brûlerai* | *J'ai brûlé* |

## bus autobus

We ride to school in a **bus**.
*Nous allons à l'école en **autobus**.*

## but mais, sauf

1. Steve pulled hard **but** the donkey would not come.
   *Steve tirait de toutes ses forces **mais** l'âne refusait d'avancer.*

2. I ate all **but** the bones.
   *J'ai tout mangé **sauf** les os.*

## butcher boucher

The **butcher** sells meat.
*Le **boucher** vend de la viande.*

## butter beurre

**Butter** is food.
*Le **beurre** est un aliment.*

It is made from cream.
*Il est fait avec de la crème.*

## button bouton

This is a green **button**.
*Voici un **bouton** vert.*

**Buttons** are used to fasten clothes.
*Les **boutons** servent à attacher les vêtements.*

## to buy acheter

Helen had a penny.
*Hélène avait une pièce de monnaie.*

She took it to **buy** sweets.
*Elle la prit pour **acheter** des bonbons.*

| I buy | I shall buy | I bought |
|-------|-------------|----------|
| *J'achète* | *J'achèterai* | *J'ai acheté* |

## by par

1. The cart was pulled **by** the horse.
   *La charrette était tirée **par** le cheval.*

2. They went to town **by** train.
   *Ils sont allés à la ville **par** le train.*

# C c

Third letter of the alphabet.
*Troisième lettre de l'alphabet.*

## cage cage

We have a canary.
*Nous avons un canari.*

We keep it in a **cage**.
*Nous le gardons dans une **cage**.*

## cake gâteau

A **cake** is sweet and good to eat.
*Un **gâteau** est sucré et bon à manger.*

Mother has baked a **cake**.
*Maman a fait un **gâteau**.*

## to call appeler

1. The children are **called** Henry and Jean.
   *Les enfants s'**appellent** Henri et Jeanne.*

2. Jean is **calling** the kitten.
   *Jeanne **appelle** le petit chat.*

| I call | I shall call | I called |
|--------|--------------|----------|
| *J'appelle* | *J'appellerai* | *J'ai appelé* |

## camera
### appareil photographique

Mother takes our pictures with a **camera**.
*Maman nous photographie avec un **appareil photographique**.*

## candle    bougie

A **candle** gives a little light.
*La **bougie** donne une faible lumière.*

The **candle** is made of wax.
*La **bougie** est en cire.*

## canoe    canoë

The redskin paddles his **canoë**.
*Le Peau-Rouge pagaie son **canoë**.*

## cap
### coiffe, casquette, capsule

| nurse's cap | hunter's cap | bottle cap |
|---|---|---|
| *coiffe* | *casquette* | *capsule* |
| *d'infirmière* | *de chasseur* | *de bouteille.* |

A **cap** is a small hat.
*Une **casquette** est un petit chapeau.*

## car    automobile, voiture

1. We sometimes call our **car** an automobile.
   *Parfois nous appelons notre voiture " **automobile** "*

## caravan    roulotte

The gypsy lives in a **caravan**.
*Le tzigane habite une **roulotte**.*

## card    carte

A **card** is a stiff piece of paper.
*Une **carte** est un morceau de papier rigide.*

1. Ruth got a post **card**.
   *Ruth a reçu une **carte** postale.*
2. We play games with **cards**.
   *Nous jouons avec des **cartes**.*

## care    soin, prudence

1. Ann takes **care** of the baby.
   *Anne prend **soin** du bébé.*
2. Tom always crosses the street with **care**.
   *Tom traverse toujours la rue avec **prudence**.*

## to carry    porter

The girls **carry** their dolls.
*Les petites filles **portent** leurs poupées.*

| I carry | I shall carry | I carried |
|---|---|---|
| *Je porte* | *Je porterai* | *J'ai porté* |

## castle    château

A **castle** is a very big house.
*Un **château** est une très grande maison.*

## cat    chat

A **cat** is an animal with fur.
*Le **chat** est un animal à fourrure.*

Our **cat** catches mice.
*Notre **chat** attrape les souris.*

## to catch    attraper
## to catch up with    rattraper

1. Ruth will **catch** the ball.
   *Ruth **attrapera** la balle.*
2. Ben is trying to **catch up with** Sue.
   *Ben essaie de **rattraper** Suzon.*

| I catch | I shall catch | I caught |
|---|---|---|
| *J'attrape* | *J'attraperai* | *J'ai attrapé* |

22

## centipede    *millepattes*

**Centipedes** have many legs.
*Les millepattes ont nombreuses pattes.*

## centre    *centre*

The hole is in the **centre** of the doughnut.
*Le trou est au centre du gâteau.*

## chain    *chaîne*

**Chains** are made of links.
*Les chaînes sont faites d'anneaux.*

## chair
## *chaise*

straight chair    rocking chair    high chair
*chaise droite*    *chaise à bascule*    *chaise d'enfant*

We sit on **chairs**.
*Nous nous asseyons sur des chaises.*

## chalk    *craie*

We write on the blackboard with **chalk**.
*Nous écrivons sur le tableau noir avec de la craie.*

## change    *monnaie*
## to change    *changer*

1. I gave 50 centimes for a 25 centimes bar of chocolate.
   *J'ai donné 50 centimes pour une barre de chocolat qui en coûtait 25.*

   The grocer gave me 25 centimes **change**.
   *L'épicier m'a rendu 25 centimes de monnaie.*

2. Patsy and Tom **change** places.
   *Patsy et Tom changent de place.*

| I change | I shall change | I changed |
|----------|----------------|-----------|
| *Je change* | *Je changerai* | *J'ai changé* |

## cheese    *fromage*

**Cheese** is food made from milk.
*Le fromage est un aliment à base de lait.*

## chest    *poitrine, commode*

1. The **chest** is a part of the body.
   *La poitrine est une partie du corps.*

   The soldier wears a medal on his **chest**.
   *Le soldat porte une médaille sur la poitrine.*

2. A **chest** is a piece of furniture.
   *Une commode est un meuble.*

   We keep our clothes in a **chest**.
   *Nous rangeons nos vêtements dans une commode.*

## chick    *poussin*

A **chick** is a baby bird.
*Un poussin est un bébé oiseau.*

The **chick** has just hatched from the egg.
*Le poussin vient de sortir de l'œuf.*

## chicken    *poulet*

Jim feeds the **chickens**.
*Jim donne à manger aux poulets.*

## chief    *chef*

A **chief** is a leader.
*Le chef est celui qui dirige.*

An Indian **chief** leads his tribe.
*Un chef indien dirige sa tribu.*

## child    *enfant*

Sammy is a **child**.
*Sammy est un enfant.*

Boys and girls are **children**.
*Les garçons et les filles sont des enfants.*

## chin    *menton*

The **chin** is a part of the face.
*Le menton est une partie du visage.*

Betty has paint on her **chin**.
*Betty a de la peinture au menton.*

## to choose   *choisir*

Tom may **choose** either chewing gum
or the sweet.
*Tom peut **choisir** le chewing-gum ou le bonbon.*

Which will he **choose?**
*Lequel **choisira**-t-il?*

| I choose | I shall choose | I chose |
|---|---|---|
| *Je choisis* | *Je choisirai* | *J'ai choisi* |

## Christmas
## *Noël*

**Christmas** is Jesus Christ's birthday.
*Le jour de **Noël** est l'anniversaire de la naissance de Jésus-Christ.*
**Christmas** is on December 25th.
*__Noël__ est le 25 décembre.*

## circle   *cercle*

A **circle** is round.
*Un **cercle** est rond.*

Jerry drew a **circle**.
*Jerry a dessiné un **cercle**.*

## circus
## *cirque*

A **circus** has trained animals and funny clowns.
*Dans un **cirque** il y a des animaux dressés et des clowns drôles.*

## city   *ville*

In a **city** there are many buildings and houses.
*Dans une **ville** il y a beaucoup de bâtiments et de maisons.*

Many people live in **cities**.
*Beaucoup de gens vivent dans des **villes**.*

## class   *classe*

These children are in a **class** in school.
*Ces enfants sont dans une **classe** à l'école.*

## clean   *propre*
## to clean   *nettoyer*

Mary's hands are **clean**.
*Les mains de Marie sont **propres**.*

She has **cleaned** them.
*Elle les a **nettoyées**.*

| I clean | I shall clean | I cleaned |
|---|---|---|
| *Je nettoie* | *Je nettoierai* | *J'ai nettoyé* |

## clear   *clair*

The water is **clear** and we can
see the fish.
*L'eau est **claire** et nous pouvons voir les poissons.*

## to climb   *grimper*

Bill is **climbing** the ladder.
*Bill **grimpe** à l'échelle.*

| I climb | I shall climb | I climbed |
|---|---|---|
| *Je grimpe* | *Je grimperai* | *J'ai grimpé* |

## clock   *pendule, horloge*

1. We tell the time by the **clock**.
   *Nous voyons l'heure à la **pendule**.*

2. The town hall has a **clock**.
   *L'hôtel de ville a une **horloge**.*

## close   *près de*
## to close   *fermer*

1. The lamb is **close** to its mother.
   *L'agneau est **près de** sa mère.*

2. Tom will **close** the door.
   *Tom **fermera** la porte.*

| I close | I shall close | I closed |
|---|---|---|
| *Je ferme* | *Je fermerai* | *J'ai fermé* |

## cloth
## *tissu, étoffe*

1. Jane's dress is made of **cloth**.
   *La robe de Jeanne est en **tissu**.*

2. **Cloth** is woven from threads.
   *L'**étoffe** est tissée avec des fils.*

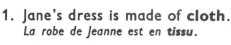

# clothes vêtements

We wear **clothes**.
*Nous portons des **vêtements**.*

The words are shown with their genders.
*Les mots sont désignés avec leur genre.*

socks
les chaussettes

nightgown
la chemise de nuit

vest
le sous-vêtement

pinafore
le tablier

stockings
les bas
(le)

coat
le manteau

hat
le chapeau

bonnet
le bonnet

sweater
le cardigan

overcoat
le pardessus

scarf
l'écharpe

pants
le caleçon

raincoat
l'imperméable
(le)

galoshes
les caoutchoucs
(le)

bib
le bavoir

pyjamas
le pyjama

skirt
la jupe

trousers
le pantalon

mittens
les moufles
(la)

shirt
la chemise

dress
la robe

shoes
les souliers (le)

slip
le jupon

bathing suit
le costume de bain

overalls
la salopette

snow suit
le costume de ski

cap
la casquette

boots
les bottes (la)

---

# cloud
## nuage

**Clouds** are found in the sky.
*Les **nuages** se trouvent dans le ciel.*

# clown    clown

A **clown** is a funny man in a circus.
*Le **clown** est un personnage comique du cirque.*

# coal    charbon

lump of coal
*morceau de charbon*

**Coal** is dug from the ground.
*Le **charbon** est extrait du sol.*

**Coal** burns and makes heat.
*Le **charbon** brûle et donne de la chaleur*

# coat
## manteau, couche

raincoat
*imperméable*

overcoat
*pardessus*

1. We wear a **coat** over other clothes.
   *Nous portons un **manteau** sur nos autres vêtements.*

2. The painter puts a **coat** of paint on the wall.
   *Le peintre applique une **couche** de peinture sur le mur.*

# cold    froid, rhume

1. **Cold** weather comes in winter.
   *Le temps **froid** vient en hiver.*

2. Ralph has a **cold**.
   *Ralph a un **rhume**.*

# collar    col, collier

man's collar
*col d'homme*

lace collar
*col de dentelle*

dog's collar
*collier de chien*

A **collar** is worn around the neck.
*Un **col** se porte autour du cou.*

25

# colour *couleur*

These are **colours**.
*Voici des **couleurs**.*

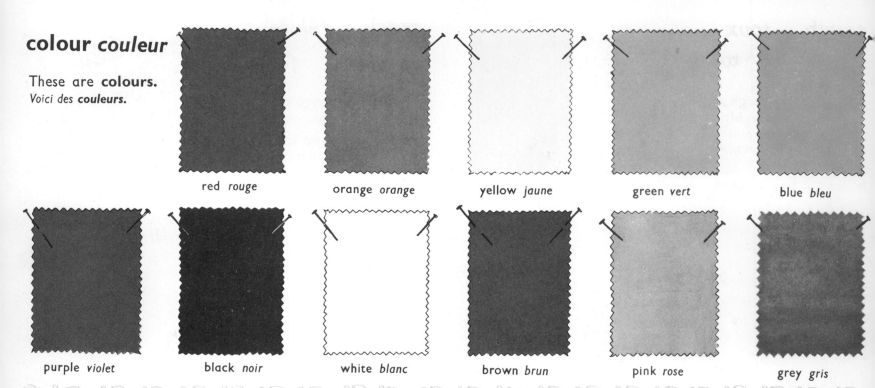

red *rouge*   orange *orange*   yellow *jaune*   green *vert*   blue *bleu*

purple *violet*   black *noir*   white *blanc*   brown *brun*   pink *rose*   grey *gris*

---

## comb   to comb
## *peigne*   *peigner*

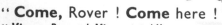

We use a **comb** to **comb** our hair.
*Nous nous servons d'un **peigne** pour **peigner** nos cheveux.*

| I comb | I shall comb | I combed |
|---|---|---|
| *Je peigne* | *Je peignerai* | *J'ai peigné* |

## to come   *venir*

" **Come**, Rover ! **Come** here ! "
*" **Viens**, Rover ! **Viens** ici ! "*

Rover **comes** to Jim.
*Rover **vient** vers Jim.*

| I come | I shall come | I came |
|---|---|---|
| *Je viens* | *Je viendrai* | *Je suis venu* |

## to cook
## *faire cuire*

Sue helps her mother to **cook** dinner.
*Suzon aide sa mère à **faire cuire** le dîner.*

| I cook | I shall cook | I cooked |
|---|---|---|
| *Je fais cuire* | *Je ferai cuire* | *J'ai fait cuire* |

## cook   *chef*

The **cook** wears a tall, white cap.
*Le **chef** porte un grand bonnet blanc.*

---

## cool   *frais*

A **cool** drink is nice in summer.
*Une boisson **fraîche** est agréable en été.*

## to copy   *copier*

We **copied** our lesson from the blackboard.
*Nous avons **copié** notre leçon d'après le tableau noir.*

| I copy | I shall copy | I copied |
|---|---|---|
| *Je copie* | *Je copierai* | *J'ai copié* |

## corn   *maïs*

This is a **corn** cob.
*Ceci est un épi de **maïs**.*

## corner   *coin*

Angus sits in the **corner**.
*Angus est assis dans le **coin**.*

## to cost   *coûter*

How much does the bar of chocolate **cost** ?
*Combien **coûte** la tablette de chocolat?*

It **costs** twenty-five centimes.
*Elle **coûte** vingt-cinq centimes.*

| It costs | It will cost | It cost |
|---|---|---|
| *Elle coûte* | *Elle coûtera* | *Elle a coûté* |

## cough    toux
## to cough    tousser

Jim took some **cough** medicine because he had been **coughing** for a week.
*Jim a pris un sirop pour la **toux** parce qu'il **toussait** depuis une semaine.*

| I cough | I shall cough | I coughed |
|---|---|---|
| *Je tousse* | *Je tousserai* | *J'ai toussé* |

## to count
## compter

We **count** the chickens.
*Nous **comptons** les poulets.*

One, two, three, four, five.
*Un, deux trois, quatre, cinq.*

| I count | I shall count | I counted |
|---|---|---|
| *Je compte* | *Je compterai* | *J'ai compté* |

## country
## campagne
## pays

1. Farms and woods are in the **country**.
   *Les fermes et les bois sont à la **campagne**.*
2. France is a **country**.
   *La France est un **pays**.*

   England is another **country**.
   *L'Angleterre est un autre **pays**.*

## cousin    cousin, cousine

1. Your **cousin** is the son of your aunt or uncle.
   *Votre **cousin** est le fils de votre tante ou de votre oncle.*
2. Jane is my **cousin**.
   *Jeanne est ma **cousine**.*

## cover    couvercle
## to cover    couvrir

| saucepan cover | box cover | bed cover |
|---|---|---|
| *couvercle de marmite* | *couvercle de boîte* | *couvertures* |

We put **covers** over things.
*Nous **couvrons** les objets avec des **couvercles**.*

| I cover | I shall cover | I covered |
|---|---|---|
| *Je couvre* | *Je couvrirai* | *J'ai couvert* |

## cow    vache

A **cow** is an animal.
*La **vache** est un animal.*

She gives us milk.
*Elle nous donne du lait.*

## crack    fêlure
## to crack    fêler

1. There is a **crack** in the cup.
   *Il y a une **fêlure** dans la tasse.*
2. Who **cracked** the cup?
   *Qui a **fêlé** la tasse?*

| I crack | I shall crack | I cracked |
|---|---|---|
| *Je fêle* | *Je fêlerai* | *J'ai fêlé* |

## cracker    diablotin, papillote

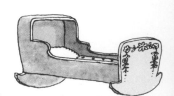

I pull the **cracker** with my sister.
*Je tire le **diablotin** avec ma sœur.*

## cradle    berceau

A **cradle** is a baby's bed.
*Un **berceau** est un lit de bébé.*

Jane rocks the baby in the **cradle**.
*Jeanne berce le bébé dans son **berceau**.*

## crayon    crayon

We draw with coloured **crayons**.
*Nous dessinons avec des **crayons** de couleur.*

## cross    croix, fâché
## to cross    traverser

1. Jack drew a red **cross** on the board.
   *Jacques a dessiné une **croix** rouge sur le tableau.*
2. The baby is **cross**. He is crying.
   *Le bébé est **fâché**. Il pleure.*
3. The dog **crosses** the street.
   *Le chien **traverse** la rue.*

| I cross | I shall cross | I crossed |
|---|---|---|
| *Je traverse* | *Je traverserai* | *J'ai traversé* |

## to cry    pleurer

We **cry** when we are unhappy.
*Nous **pleurons** quand nous sommes malheureux.*

| I cry | I shall cry | I cried |
|---|---|---|
| *Je pleure* | *Je pleurerai* | *J'ai pleuré* |

## cup    tasse

I have a **cup** of milk.
*J'ai une **tasse** de lait.*

## cupboard
## armoire

The **cupboard** is full.
*L'armoire est pleine.*

## curl **boucle**
## to curl **friser**

1. The pig has a **curl** in its tail.
   *Le cochon a une **boucle** à la queue.*
2. Mary's mother **curls** her hair.
   *La mère de Marie lui **frise** les cheveux.*

| I curl | I shall curl | I curled |
|--------|--------------|----------|
| *Je frise* | *Je friserai* | *J'ai frisé* |

## to cut **couper**
## **se couper**

1. Susan **cut** her finger.
   *Suzanne s'est **coupé** le doigt.*

2. Scissors and knives are for **cutting**.
   *Les ciseaux et les couteaux servent à **couper**.*

| I cut | I shall cut | I cut |
|-------|-------------|-------|
| *Je coupe* | *Je couperai* | *J'ai coupé* |

# D d

Fourth letter of the alphabet.
*Quatrième lettre de l'alphabet.*

## daddy **papa**

I call my father **Daddy**.
*J'appelle mon père **Papa**.*

## to dance **danser**

We **dance** to the sound of music.
*Nous **dansons** au son de la musique.*

| I dance | I shall dance | I danced |
|---------|---------------|----------|
| *Je danse* | *Je danserai* | *J'ai dansé* |

## danger **danger**

The sign says **Danger**.
*L'écriteau dit **Danger**.*

## dark
## sombre
## obscurité

1. These are **dark** colours.
   *Voici des couleurs **sombres**.*
2. We cannot see in the **dark**.
   *Nous ne pouvons pas voir dans l'**obscurité**.*

## daughter
## fille

Jane is the **daughter** of her father and her mother.
*Jeanne est la **fille** de son père et de sa mère.*

## day **jour, journée**

1. The **day** comes after the night.
   *Le **jour** vient après la nuit.*

   The seven **days** of the week are Monday, Tuesday, Wednesday, Thursday, Friday, Saturday and Sunday.
   *Les sept **jours** de la semaine sont: lundi, mardi, mercredi, jeudi, vendredi, samedi et dimanche.*

2. It was a lovely **day**.
   *C'était une belle **journée**.*

## dead **mort**

**Dead** means not living any more.
*Mort signifie qui ne vit plus.*
The flower is **dead**.
*La fleur est **morte**.*

## deep **profond**

We dug a **deep** hole in the ground.
*Nous avons creusé un trou **profond** dans le sol.*

## dentist   *dentiste*

A **dentist** takes care of our teeth.
*Le **dentiste** soigne nos dents.*

## desk   *bureau*

A **desk** holds papers and pencils.
*Le **bureau** contient des papiers et des crayons.*

Helen keeps her **desk** tidy.
*Hélène garde son **bureau** en ordre.*

## to destroy   *détruire*

The storm **destroys** the bridge.
*La tempête **détruit** le pont.*

| I destroy | I shall destroy | I destroyed |
|---|---|---|
| *Je détruis* | *Je détruirai* | *J'ai détruit* |

## dictionary   *dictionnaire*

A **dictionary** teaches the meaning of words.
*Un **dictionnaire** enseigne la signification des mots.*

This book is a **dictionary**.
*Ce livre est un **dictionnaire**.*

## different   *différent*

These flowers are **different**.
*Ces fleurs sont **différentes**.*

## to dig   *creuser*

I **dig** a hole with my spade.
*Je **creuse** un trou avec ma bêche.*

| I dig | I shall dig | I dug |
|---|---|---|
| *Je creuse* | *Je creuserai* | *J'ai creusé* |

## dinner   *dîner*

**Dinner** is the biggest meal of the day.
*Le **dîner** est le plus grand repas de la journée.*

## direction   *direction*

The signpost points the **direction**.
*Le poteau indicateur indique la **direction**.*

## discover   *découvrir*

Christopher Columbus **discovered** America.
*Christophe Colomb **a découvert** l'Amérique.*

## dish   *plat*

The **dish** is blue.
*Le **plat** est bleu.*

Our meals are served in **dishes**.
*Nos mets sont servis dans des **plats**.*

## distance   *distance*

The farm is a long **distance** from the town.
*La ferme est à une longue **distance** de la ville.*

## to divide   *partager, diviser*

Mother will **divide** the pie.
*Maman va **partager** la tarte.*

| I divide | I shall divide | I divided |
|---|---|---|
| *Je partage* | *Je partagerai* | *J'ai partagé* |
| *Je divise* | *Je diviserai* | *J'ai divisé* |

## to do    *faire*

1 What does an aeroplane **do**?
*Que fait un avion ?*

It flies.
*Il vole.*

2. What is Bobby **doing**?
*Que fait Bobby ?*

He is painting a chest.
*Il peint une commode.*

| I do | I shall do | I did |
|------|-----------|-------|
| *Je fais* | *Je ferai* | *J'ai fait* |

## doctor    *médecin*

The **doctor** takes care of us when we are ill.
*Le médecin nous soigne quand nous sommes malades.*

## dog    *chien*

A **dog** is an animal.
*Le chien est un animal.*

**Dogs** make good pets.
*Les chiens font de bons amis.*

## doll    *poupée*

A **doll** is a toy.
*Une poupée est un jouet.*

Ruth's **doll** is dressed like a baby.
*La poupée de Ruth est habillée comme un bébé.*

## dollar    *dollar*

A **dollar** is American money.
*Le dollar est une monnaie américaine.*

In 1960, a **dollar** was worth about five francs.
*En 1960, un dollar valait environ cinq francs.*

## door    *porte*

The **door** is open.
*La porte est ouverte.*

## downstairs    *en bas*

Mother is **downstairs** and Father upstairs.
*Maman est en bas et papa en haut.*

## to draw    *tirer, dessiner*

1. The horse **draws** the cart.
*Le cheval tire la charrette.*

2. Bill likes to **draw** pictures.
*Bill aime dessiner des images.*

| I draw | I shall draw | I drew |
|--------|-------------|--------|
| *Je tire* | *Je tirerai* | *J'ai tiré* |
| *Je dessine* | *Je dessinerai* | *J'ai dessiné* |

## dream    *rêve*
## to dream    *rêver*

1. Can you remember your **dreams**?
*Pouvez-vous vous rappeler vos rêves ?*

2. Sometimes we **dream** in our sleep.
*Quelquefois nous rêvons pendant notre sommeil.*

| I dream | I shall dream | I dreamed |
|---------|--------------|-----------|
| *Je rêve* | *Je rêverai* | *J'ai rêvé* |

## dress    *robe*

Patsy has a yellow **dress**.
*Patsy a une robe jaune.*

Girls and women wear **dresses**.
*Les petites filles et les femmes portent des robes.*

## drink    *boisson*
## to drink    *boire*

1. Milk is a **drink**.
*Le lait est une boisson.*

2. Tom is **drinking** a glass of milk.
*Tom boit un verre de lait.*

| I drink | I shall drink | I drank |
|---------|--------------|---------|
| *Je bois* | *Je boirai* | *J'ai bu* |

## to drive    *conduire*
## driver    *conducteur*

Father **drives** our car.
*Papa conduit notre voiture.*

He is the **driver**.
*Il est le conducteur.*

| I drive | I shall drive | I drove |
|---------|--------------|---------|
| *Je conduis* | *Je conduirai* | *J'ai conduit* |

## drop    goutte
## to drop    tomber

A **drop** of rain **dropped** on the window sill.

*Une **goutte** de pluie est **tombée** sur le bord de la fenêtre.*

| It drops | It will drop | It dropped |
|----------|--------------|------------|
| *Elle tombe* | *Elle tombera* | *Elle est tombée* |

## drum    tambour

We beat a **drum** with drumsticks.
*Nous jouons du **tambour** avec des baguettes.*

## dry    sec
## to dry    sécher

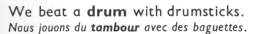

1. The wet clothes will soon be dry.
   *Les habits mouillés seront bientôt **secs**.*

2. The clothes are **drying** on the line.
   *Les habits **sèchent** sur la corde.*

| I dry | I shall dry | I dried |
|-------|-------------|---------|
| *Je sèche* | *Je sècherai* | *J'ai séché* |

## duck
## canard

**Ducks** are birds that live near water.

*Les **canards** sont des oiseaux qui vivent près de l'eau.*

They swim and fly.
*Ils nagent et volent.*

## during    pendant

**During** the shower we stayed indoors.
*Pendant l'averse nous sommes restés à l'intérieur.*

## dust    poussière
## to dust    épousseter

1. Mother takes off the **dust** with a **duster.**

   *Maman enlève la **poussière** avec un **chiffon à poussière**.*

2. She **dusts** the chair.
   *Elle **époussète** la chaise.*

| I dust | I shall dust | I dusted |
|--------|--------------|----------|
| *J'époussète* | *J'époussèterai* | *J'ai épousseté* |

# E e

Fifth letter of the alphabet.
*Cinquième lettre de l'alphabet.*

## each
## chaque

There is a spoon on **each** plate.
*Il y a une cuillère sur **chaque** assiette.*

## ear    oreille, épi

1. Our **ears** are for hearing.
   *Nos **oreilles** servent à entendre.*

2. An **ear** of corn grows on the stalk.
   *Un **épi** de maïs pousse sur la tige.*

## early    tôt

The cock crows **early** in the morning.
*Le coq chante **tôt** le matin.*

## earth    terre

1. We plant seeds in the **earth.**
   *Nous plantons des graines dans la **terre**.*

2. **Earth** is a planet.
   *La **terre** est une planète.*

## east    est

**East** is a direction.
*L'**est** est une direction.*

The sun comes up in the **east.**
*Le soleil se lève à l'**est**.*

## easy　*facile*

It is **easy** to slide down.
*Il est facile de descendre en glissant.*

It is not **easy** to climb up.
*Il n'est pas facile de grimper.*

## to eat　*manger*

We **eat** our food.
*Nous mangeons notre nourriture.*

Last night we **ate** chicken.
*Hier soir nous avons mangé du poulet.*

| I eat | I shall eat | I ate |
|-------|-------------|-------|
| *Je mange* | *Je mangerai* | *J'ai mangé* |

## edge　*bord*

The handkerchief has a lace **edge**.
*Le mouchoir a un bord en dentelle.*

## egg　*œuf*

There is a bird's **egg** in the nest.
*Il y a un œuf d'oiseau dans le nid.*

We eat hens' **eggs**.
*Nous mangeons des œufs de poules.*

## eight　*huit*

**Eight** is a number.
*Huit est un nombre.*

Here are **eight** candles.
*Voici huit bougies.*

## either......or
## soit......soit

Sam may take **either** the big book **or** the little book.
*Sam peut prendre soit le gros livre, soit le petit livre.*

## electric　*électrique*

We have **electric** lights, an **electric** iron and an **electric** fan.

*Nous avons des lampes électriques, un fer électrique et un ventilateur électrique.*

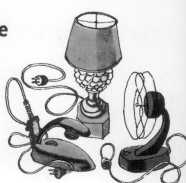

## else　*d'autre*

1. Will you take anything **else**?
   *Prendrez-vous quelque chose d'autre?*

2. Who **else** will play on our side?
   *Qui d'autre va jouer dans notre camp?*

## empty　*vide*

The pail is **empty**.
*Le seau est vide.*

## end　*fin, bout*

1. The **end** of the book.
   *La fin du livre.*

2. Ruth is at the **end** of the line.
   *Ruth est au bout du rang.*

## engine
## locomotive
## moteur

1. This **engine** pulls the train.
   *Cette locomotive tire le train.*

2. A plane has **engines**.
   *L'avion a des moteurs.*

## to enjoy　*aimer*

We **enjoy** playing in the sand.
*Nous aimons jouer dans le sable.*

| I enjoy | I shall enjoy | I enjoyed |
|---------|---------------|-----------|
| *J'aime* | *J'aimerai* | *J'ai aimé* |

## enough   *assez*

There is not **enough** ribbon to go around the parcel.
*Il n'y a pas **assez** de ruban pour entourer le paquet.*

Tom is tall **enough** to reach the shelf.
*Tom est **assez** grand pour atteindre l'étagère.*

## to enter   *entrer*

We **entered** the church.
*Nous sommes **entrés** dans l'église.*

| I enter | I shall enter | I entered |
|---------|---------------|-----------|
| *J'entre* | *J'entrerai* | *Je suis entré* |

## envelope   *enveloppe*

A letter is in the **envelope**.
*Il y a une lettre dans l'**enveloppe**.*

## equal   *égal*

The cake is cut in **equal** parts.
*Le gâteau est coupé en parts **égales**.*

## error   *erreur*

$$2 + 2 = \cancel{5}$$

Peter said that two and two make five.
*Pierre a dit que deux et deux font cinq.*

Peter made an **error**.
*Pierre a fait une **erreur**.*

$$2 + 2 = 4$$

## even

### même, de façon égale, pair

1. The dog runs **even** when he is tired.
   *Le chien court **même** quand il est fatigué.*

2. Jane folds the edges **even**.
   *Jeanne plie les bords **de façon égale**.*

3. Two, four, six are **even** numbers.
   *Deux, quatre, six sont des nombres **pairs**.*

## evening

### soir, soirée

1. **Evening** is the end of the day.
   *Le **soir** est la fin du jour.*

2. In the **evening** it grows dark.
   *Dans la **soirée** il fait sombre.*

## ever   *jamais*

Were you **ever** late?
*Avez-vous **jamais** été en retard?*

## every

### chaque

**Every** dog has a tail.
***Chaque** chien a une queue.*

## everything   *tout*

Did you eat **everything** that was on your plate?
*Avez-vous mangé **tout** ce qui était dans votre assiette?*

## except

### sauf

All the children went to school **except** the baby.
*Tous les enfants sont allés à l'école, **sauf** le bébé.*

## to expect   *attendre*

We **expect** to see the circus.
*Nous **attendons** de voir le cirque.*

| I expect | I shall expect | I expected |
|----------|----------------|------------|
| *J'attends* | *J'attendrai* | *J'ai attendu* |

## eye   *œil, chas*

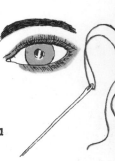

1. We see with our **eyes**.
   *Nous voyons avec nos **yeux**.*

2. Thread goes through the **eye** of a needle.
   *Le fil passe par le **chas** de l'aiguille.*

# F f

Sixth letter of the alphabet.
*Sixième lettre de l'alphabet.*

## face   *visage*

Timothy has a smiling **face**.
*Timothée a le **visage** souriant.*

## fact   *fait*

A **fact** is something we know.
*Un **fait** est quelque chose que nous savons.*

Two and two make four.
*Deux et deux font quatre.*

This is a **fact**.
*C'est un **fait**.*

## fair   *juste*

This is a **fair** rule.
*Ce règlement est **juste**.*

## fair
## *foire*

The little pig went to the **fair**.
*Le petit cochon est allé à la **foire**.*

## fairy   *fée*

Jane believes in **fairies**.
*Jeanne croit aux **fées**.*

Do you like **fairy** tales?
*Aimez-vous les contes de **fées**?*

## to fall   *tomber*

Sam is going to **fall**.
*Sam va **tomber**.*

Whoops! There he goes.
*Pouf! Le voilà qui **tombe**.*

| I fall | I shall fall | I fell |
|---|---|---|
| *Je tombe* | *Je tomberai* | *Je suis tombé* |

## false   *faux*

**False** means not true.
***Faux** signifie pas vrai.*

It is **false** to say that the sun rises in the evening.
*Il est **faux** de dire que le soleil se lève le soir.*

## family   *famille*

Parents and children make a **family**.
*Les parents et les enfants forment une **famille**.*

The **family** is out walking.
*La **famille** est sortie se promener.*

## fan   *éventail*

A **fan** is used to keep us cool.
*L'**éventail** sert à nous rafraîchir.*

## far

## *loin*

The school is near the house.
*L'école est près de la maison.*

The church is **far** from the house.
*L'église est **loin** de la maison.*

The bank is **farther** away.
*La banque est **plus loin** encore.*

The shop is **farthest** from the house.
*C'est la boutique qui se trouve **le plus loin** de la maison.*

## farm   *ferme*

Farmer Brown lives on a **farm**.
*Le fermier Lebrun habite dans une **ferme**.*

He grows vegetables and fruit.
*Il fait pousser des légumes et des fruits.*

## fast     vite, rapide

1. Bob ran **fast**.
   *Bob courait **vite**.*
   He won the race.
   *Il a gagné la course.*
2. He is a **fast** runner.
   *C'est un coureur **rapide**.*

## fat     gras

The pink pig is **fat**.
*Le cochon rose est **gras**.*
The black pig is not **fat**.
*Le cochon noir n'est pas **gras**.*

## father     père

The **father** is head of the family.
*Le **père** est le chef de la famille.*

## feather     plume

Birds are covered with **feathers**.
*Les oiseaux sont couverts de **plumes**.*

## to feed     nourrir

Watch Peter **feed** the pigeons.
*Regardez Pierre **nourrir** les pigeons.*

| I feed | I shall feed | I fed |
| --- | --- | --- |
| *Je nourris* | *Je nourrirai* | *J'ai nourri* |

## to feel

### sentir, se sentir

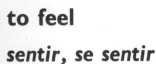

1. Jane **feels** the cat's soft fur.
   *Jeanne **sent** la douce fourrure du chat.*
2. Bob is not **feeling** well.
   *Bob ne **se sent** pas bien.*

| I feel | I shall feel | I felt |
| --- | --- | --- |
| *Je sens* | *Je sentirai* | *J'ai senti* |

## fence

## grille

The **fence** encloses the garden.
*La **grille** entoure le jardin.*

## few

### quelques

There are **a few** eggs in the nest.
*Il y a **quelques** œufs dans le nid.*

## field     champ

The **field** has trees at the edges.
*Le **champ** est bordé d'arbres.*

## fifteen

### quinze     **15**

Fifteen is a number.
*Quinze est un nombre.*
Ten and five make **fifteen**.
*Dix et cinq font **quinze**.*

## fifty     cinquante     **50**

Fifty is a number.
*Cinquante est un nombre.*
Five tens make **fifty**.
*Cinq fois dix font **cinquante**.*

$$5 \times 10 = 50$$

## to fight

### se battre

A soldier **fights**.
*Un soldat **se bat**.*

| I fight | I shall fight | I fought |
| --- | --- | --- |
| *Je me bats* | *Je me battrai* | *Je me suis battu* |

## figure     chiffre, figure

1. We write numbers with **figures**.
   *Nous écrivons les nombres avec des **chiffres**.*
2. The girl is **figure** skating.
   *La petite fille fait des **figures** de patinage.*

## to fill     remplir

I **fill** the pail with water.
*Je **remplis** le seau d'eau.*

| I fill | I shall fill | I filled |
| --- | --- | --- |
| *Je remplis* | *Je remplirai* | *J'ai rempli* |

## to find    trouver

Judy cannot **find** her shoe.
*Judy ne peut pas **trouver** son soulier.*

She has looked for it everywhere.
*Elle l'a cherché partout.*

| I find | I shall find | I found |
|---|---|---|
| *Je trouve* | *Je trouverai* | *J'ai trouvé* |

## finger    doigt

A **finger** is a part of the hand.
*Le **doigt** est une partie de la main.*

Bill points with his **finger**.
*Bill montre avec son **doigt**.*

## to finish    finir

Mother read us part of a story.
*Maman nous a lu une partie d'une histoire.*

Today she will **finish** it.
*Aujourd'hui elle la **finira**.*

| I finish | I shall finish | I finished |
|---|---|---|
| *Je finis* | *Je finirai* | *J'ai fini* |

## fire    feu

A **fire** burns and gives light and heat.
*Le **feu** brûle et donne lumière et chaleur.*

We made a little **fire**.
*Nous avons fait un petit **feu**.*

## first    premier

Mary sits in the **first** seat.
*Marie est assise au **premier** rang.*

A is the **first** letter of the alphabet.
*A est la **première** lettre de l'alphabet.*

## fish    poisson     to fish    pêcher

1. **Fish** live in the water.
   *Les **poissons** vivent dans l'eau.*
2. These boys are **fishing**.
   *Ces garçons **pêchent**.*

| I fish | I shall fish | I fished |
|---|---|---|
| *Je pêche* | *Je pêcherai* | *J'ai pêché* |

## five    5

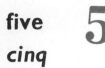

### cinq

Five is a number.
*Cinq est un nombre.*

Here are **five** little pigs.
*Voici **cinq** petits cochons.*

## flag    drapeau

The **flag** waves in the wind.
*Le **drapeau** claque dans le vent.*

This is the **flag** of Great Britain.
*Voici le **drapeau** de la Grande-Bretagne.*

## flame    flamme

A **flame** is bright and hot.
*La **flamme** est brillante et chaude.*

## flat    plat

The roof is **flat**.
*Le toit est **plat**.*

## to float

### flotter

Boats **float** on the water.
*Les bateaux **flottent** sur l'eau.*

| I float | I shall float | I floated |
|---|---|---|
| *Je flotte* | *Je flotterai* | *J'ai flotté* |

## floor    plancher

The rug is on the **floor**.
*Le tapis est sur le **plancher**.*

## flour    farine

Mother made a cake.
*Maman a fait un gâteau.*

She used **flour**.
*Elle a employé de la **farine**.*

**Flour** is made from wheat.
*La **farine** est faite avec du blé.*

# flower    *fleur*

Some plants have **flowers**.
*Certaines plantes ont des **fleurs**.*

These are **flowers**.
*Voici des **fleurs**.*

geranium
*le géranium*

carnation
*l'œillet (le)*

daisy
*la marguerite*

daffodil
*la jonquille*

petunia
*le pétunia*

tulip
*la tulipe*

lily
*le lys*

violet
*la violette*

pansy
*la pensée*

rose
*la rose*

orchid
*l'orchidée (la)*

poppy
*le coquelicot*

gardenia
*le gardénia*

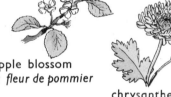

buttercup
*le bouton d'or*

lily-of-the-valley
*le muguet*

dog-rose
*l'églantine (la)*

ladyslipper
*le sabot de la vierge*

lilac
*le lilas*

apple blossom
*la fleur de pommier*

chrysanthemum
*le chrysanthème*

jack-in-the-pulpit
*l'arum pied-de-veau (le)*

# fly            to fly

# mouche        voler

1. A **fly** is an insect which can **fly**.
   *Une **mouche** est un insecte qui peut **voler**.*

2. Birds and aeroplanes can **fly**.
   *Les oiseaux et les avions peuvent **voler**.*

| I fly | I shall fly | I flew |
|---|---|---|
| *Je vole* | *Je volerai* | *J'ai volé* |

---

# to fold    *plier*

Can you **fold** a handkerchief?
*Savez-vous **plier** un mouchoir ?*

| I fold | I shall fold | I folded |
|---|---|---|
| *Je plie* | *Je plierai* | *J'ai plié* |

# to follow      suivre

The kitten **follows** its mother.
*Le chaton **suit** sa mère.*

| I follow | I shall follow | I followed |
|---|---|---|
| *Je suis* | *Je suivrai* | *J'ai suivi* |

# food      *aliment, nourriture*

We eat **food**.
*Nous mangeons de la **nourriture**.*

Here is some **food**.
*Voici quelques **aliments**.*

Try to learn their genders.
*Essayez d'apprendre leurs genres.*

chop
*la côtelette*

roast beef
*le rôti de bœuf*

chicken
*le poulet*

sausages
*les saucisses (la)*

cake
*le gâteau*

bread
*le pain*

butter
*le beurre*

celery
*le céleri*

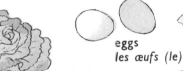

eggs
*les œufs (le)*

fish
*le poisson*

lettuce
*la laitue*

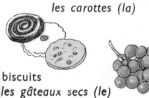

carrots
*les carottes (la)*

sugar
*le sucre*

beans
*les haricots (le)*

jam
*la confiture*

biscuits
*les gâteaux secs (le)*

cheese
*le fromage*

grapes
*les raisins (le)*

biscuits
*les biscuits (le)*

ice cream
*la glace*

milk
*le lait*

potato
*la pomme de terre*

tomato
*la tomate*

porridge
*la bouillie*

apple
*la pomme*

soup
*la soupe*

pie
*la tarte*

37

## foot    *pied*

1. A **foot** is a part of the body.
   *Le **pied** est une partie du corps.*

   Each **foot** has five toes.
   *Chaque **pied** a cinq orteils.*

   We stand on our two **feet**.
   *Nous nous tenons debout sur nos deux **pieds**.*

2. The rug is at the **foot** of the stairs.
   *Le tapis est au **pied** de l'escalier.*

## for    *pour*

It is a good day **for** a picnic.
*C'est une excellente journée **pour** un pique-nique.*

I gave twenty-five centimes **for** a bar of chocolate.
*J'ai donné vingt cinq centimes **pour** une tablette de chocolat.*

I washed the dishes **for** my mother.
*J'ai fait la vaisselle **pour** Maman.*

## forest    *forêt*

Red Riding Hood went into the **forest**.
*Le petit Chaperon Rouge entra dans la **forêt**.*

Many trees make a **forest**.
*Beaucoup d'arbres forment une **forêt**.*

## fork    *fourchette*

I eat with a **fork**.
*Je mange avec une **fourchette**.*

## four    *quatre*

**Four** is a number.
***Quatre** est un nombre.*

There are **four** marbles.
*Il y a **quatre** billes.*

## fox    *renard*

A **fox** is an animal.
*Un **renard** est un animal.*

## free    *libre, gratuit*
## to free    *libérer*

1. We **freed** the bird.
   *Nous avons **libéré** l'oiseau.*

2. Now it is **free** to go.
   *Maintenant il est **libre** de partir.*

3. The sweets were **free**.
   *Les bonbons étaient **gratuits**.*

| I free | I shall free | I freed |
|--------|--------------|---------|
| *Je libère* | *Je libèrerai* | *J'ai libéré* |

## friend    *ami*

Helen and Grace are **friends**.
*Hélène et Grâce sont **amies**.*

## from    *de, depuis*

1. Rover runs **from** Bob to Ann.
   *Rover court **de** Bob vers Anne.*

   Smoke is coming **from** the chimney.
   *La fumée sort **de** la cheminée.*

   The train leaves **from** Paris.
   *Le train part **de** Paris.*

2. **From** that day on they lived happily.
   ***Depuis** ce jour ils vécurent heureux.*

## front    *devant*

A coat opens down the **front**.
*Un manteau s'ouvre par **devant**.*

Mary ran in through the **front** door.
*Marie est entrée en courant par la porte de **devant**.*

# fruit  *fruits*

Many **fruits** are good to eat.
*Beaucoup de **fruits** sont bons à manger.*

These are **fruits**.
*Voici des **fruits**.*

banana
*la banane*

orange
*l'orange*

cherries
*les cerises
(la)*

strawberries
*les fraises
(la)*

pineapple
*l'ananas
(le)*

melon
*le melon*

apple
*la pomme*

lemon
*le citron*

plum
*la prune*

raspberry
*la framboise*

peach
*la pêche*

pear
*la poire*

gooseberry
*la groseille
à maquereau*

blueberries
*les myrtilles (la)*

grapefruit
*le pamplemousse*

grapes
*les raisins (le)*

watermelon
*la pastèque*

# full  *plein*

The basket is **full**.
*Le panier est **plein**.*

# to have fun  *s'amuser*

The children are **having fun**.
*Les enfants **s'amusent**.*

I have fun
*Je m'amuse*

I shall have fun
*Je m'amuserai*

I had fun
*Je me suis amusé*

# funny  *comique, drôle*

1. The clown was **funny**; he made us laugh.
   *Le clown était **comique**; il nous a fait rire.*

2. What a **funny** thing!
   *Quelle **drôle** de chose !*

# fur
*fourrure*

Some animals have **fur**.
*Certains animaux ont une **fourrure**.*

# furniture
*mobilier, meubles*

1. We have **furniture** in the house.
   *Nous avons un **mobilier** dans la maison.*

2. This is **furniture**.
   *Voici des **meubles**.*

lamp
*la lampe*

bed
*le lit*

armchair
*le fauteuil*

straight chair
*la chaise*

desk
*le bureau*

stool
*le tabouret*

table
*la table*

clock
*la pendule*

buffet
*le buffet*

rocking chair
*la chaise à bascule*

carpet
*le tapis*

mirror
*le miroir*

chest
*la commode*

bookcase
*la bibliothèque*

sofa
*le canapé*

# G g

Seventh letter of the alphabet.
*Septième lettre de l'alphabet.*

## game    *jeu*

The boys are playing a **game**.
*Les garçons jouent a un jeu.*

## garage    *garage*

We keep the car in the **garage**.
*Nous rangeons la voiture dans le garage.*

## garden
*jardin*

Plants and flowers grow in the **garden**.
*Des plantes et des fleurs poussent dans le jardin.*

## gas    *gaz*

1. We have a **gas** stove for cooking.
   *Nous avons un fourneau à gaz pour faire la cuisine.*
2. Balloons are filled with **gas**.
   *Les ballons sont remplis de gaz.*

## to gasp    *avoir le souffle coupé*

## gate    *portail*

A **gate** is a doorway in a fence or wall.
*Un portail est un passage dans une clôture ou dans un mur.*

## to get
### *aller chercher, recevoir*

1. Judy will **get** the biscuits.
   *Judy ira chercher les biscuits.*
2. Henry **got** a letter.
   *Henri a reçu une lettre.*

| I get | I shall get | I got |
|---|---|---|
| *Je vais chercher* | *J'irai chercher* | *Je suis allé chercher* |
| *Je reçois* | *Je recevrai* | *J'ai reçu* |

## to get up    *se lever*

Are the children **getting up** ?
*Les enfants se lèvent-ils ?*

| I get up | I shall get up | I got up |
|---|---|---|
| *Je me lève* | *Je me lèverai* | *Je me suis levé* |

## giant    *géant*

Jack met a **giant**.
*Jacques a rencontré un géant.*

The **giant** was a very big man.
*Le géant était un homme très grand.*

## gift    *cadeau*

Santa Claus gave Mary Ellen a **gift**.
*Le Père Noël a fait un cadeau à Marie-Hélène.*

## girl    *fille*

Jane is a **girl**.
*Jeanne est une fille.*

## to give    *donner*

Mother **gives** Bob a gift.
*Maman donne un cadeau à Bob.*

| I give | I shall give | I gave |
|---|---|---|
| *Je donne* | *Je donnerai* | *J'ai donné* |

## glad    content

The dog is **glad** to see his master.
*Le chien est **content** de voir son maître.*

## glass    verre, lunettes

1. Windows are made of **glass**.
   *Les fenêtres sont en **verre**.*

   We drink from a **glass**.
   *Nous buvons dans un **verre**.*

2. Grandmother wears **glasses**, to help her see better.
   *Grand-mère porte des **lunettes**, pour l'aider à mieux voir.*

## glove    gant

We wear **gloves** on our hands.
*Nous portons des **gants** aux mains.*

## to go    aller

Edith **goes** to the shop.
*Edith **va** à la boutique.*

| I go | I shall go | I went |
|------|-----------|--------|
| *Je vais* | *J'irai* | *Je suis allé* |

## goat    chèvre

A **goat** is an animal.
*La **chèvre** est un animal.*

**Goats** give milk.
*Les **chèvres** donnent du lait.*

## God    Dieu

**God** is our Father in Heaven.
*Dieu est notre Père dans le ciel.*

## gold    or

**Gold** is a yellow metal.
*L'**or** est un métal jaune.*

## golden    doré

Ann has **golden** curls.
*Anne a des boucles **dorées**.*

## good    bon

Mary is a **good** girl.
*Marie est une **bonne** fille.*

Cookies taste **good**.
*Les biscuits ont **bon** goût.*

## good
bon

This is a **good** apple.
*Voici une **bonne** pomme.*

This is a **better** apple.
*Cette pomme est **meilleure**.*

This is the **best** apple.
*Cette pomme est **la meilleure** des trois.*

## good-bye    adieu, au revoir

1. They are waving **good-bye**.
   *Ils font un signe **adieu**.*

2. They say **good-bye** before going to school.
   *Ils disent **au revoir** avant d'aller à l'école.*

## grain    grain

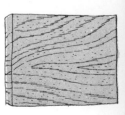

1. Tom let the **grains** of sand fall through his hand.
   *Tom laissa tomber les **grains** de sable entre ses doigts.*

   **Grains** of sand are like small seeds.
   *Les **grains** de sable sont semblables à de petites graines.*

2. The **grain** of wood is shown by the lines in it.
   *Les lignes révèlent le **grain** du bois.*

# grandfather
## grand-père

My mother's father is called **grandfather**.
*Le père de ma mère s'appelle Grand-père*

My father's father is called **grandfather**.
*Le père de mon père s'appelle Grand-père.*

# grandmother
## grand-mère

My mother's mother is called **grandmother**.
*La mère de ma mère s'appelle Grand-mère*

My father's mother is called **grandmother**.
*La mère de mon père s'appelle Grand-mère*

# grape    *raisin*

**Grapes** are fruit.
*Les **raisins** sont des fruits.*

They grow in bunches on a vine.
*Ils poussent en grappes sur une vigne.*

# grass    *herbe*

The **grass** covers the ground.
*L'**herbe** couvre le sol.*

# great    *grand*

1. The **great** mountain is very high.
   *La **grande** montagne est très élevée.*
2. President Lincoln was a **great** man.
   *Le président Lincoln était un **grand** homme.*

# green    *vert*

**Green** is a colour.
*Le **vert** est une couleur.*

Grass is **green**.
*L'herbe est **verte**.*

# grocer    *épicier*

The **grocer** sells food.
*L'**épicier** vend des aliments.*

The **grocer** sells **groceries**.
*L'**épicier** vend de l'**épicerie**.*

# ground    *sol*

Plants grow in the **ground**.
*Les plantes poussent dans le sol.*

# group    *groupe*

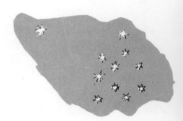

One star is by itself.
*Une étoile est toute seule.*

The others are in a **group**.
*Les autres sont en **groupe**.*

# to grow    *grandir    pousser*

My little rabbit will **grow**.
*Mon petit lapin **grandira**.*

| I grow | I shall grow | I grew |
|---|---|---|
| *Je grandis* | *Je grandirai* | *J'ai grandi* |

# to guess    *deviner*

**Guess** where Tim is hiding.
***Devinez** où Tim se cache.*

| I guess | I shall guess | I guessed |
|---|---|---|
| *Je devine* | *Je devinerai* | *J'ai deviné* |

# guide    *guide*
# to guide    *guider*

The **guide** takes us fishing.
*Le **guide** nous emmène pêcher.*

He **guides** us up the river.
*Il nous **guide** le long de la rivière.*

| I guide | I shall guide | I guided |
|---|---|---|
| *Je guide* | *Je guiderai* | *J'ai guidé* |

# gun    *fusil*

**Guns** are used for hunting.
*Les **fusils** servent à chasser.*

# H h

Eighth letter of the alphabet.
*Huitième lettre de l'alphabet.*

## hair    *cheveux, poil*

1. We have **hair** on our heads.
   *Nous avons des **cheveux** sur la tête.*

2. A dog is covered with **hair**.
   *Le chien est couvert de **poils**.*

## half    *moitié    demi*

The pie is cut in **half**.
*La tarte est coupée par la **moitié**.*

The two **halves** are the same size.
*Les deux **moitiés** sont de la même taille.*

## Hallowe'en
## *Hallowe'en*

**Hallowe'en** is the evening before All Saints' Day.
*Hallowe'en est la veille de la Toussaint.*

In the United States children dress as witches and carry Jack-o'-lanterns on **Hallowe'en**.
*Aux Etats-Unis les enfants se déguisent en sorcières et portent des lampions le soir de Hallowe'en.*

## hammer
## *marteau*

A **hammer** is used for hitting nails.
*Un **marteau** sert à enfoncer des clous.*

## hand    *main, aiguille*

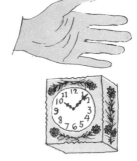

1. My **hand** has five fingers.
   *Ma **main** a cinq doigts.*

2. A clock has two **hands** that show the time.
   *Une pendule a deux **aiguilles** qui indiquent l'heure.*

## handkerchief
## *mouchoir*

I carry a **handkerchief** to blow my nose.
*Je prends un **mouchoir** pour me moucher.*

## handle    *poignée*

We hold things by the **handles**.
*Nous tenons les objets par la **poignée**.*

## to hang
## *pendre, suspendre*

The coat **hangs** on the hook.
*Le manteau **pend** au crochet.*

| I hang | I shall hang | I hung |
|---|---|---|
| *Je pends* | *Je pendrai* | *J'ai pendu* |
| *Je suspends* | *Je suspendrai* | *J'ai suspendu* |

## to happen    *arriver*

What will **happen**?
*Qu'**arrivera**-t-il ?*

| It happens | It will happen | It happened |
|---|---|---|
| *Il arrive* | *Il arrivera* | *Il est arrivé* |

## happy    *heureux*

We are all **happy** at Christmas.
*Nous sommes tous **heureux** à Noël.*

Jim has a **happy** face.
*Jim a le visage **heureux**.*

## hard    *dur*

1. Stones are **hard**.
   *Les pierres sont **dures**.*

2. The farmer works **hard**.
   *Le fermier travaille **dur**.*

## hat    *chapeau*

A **hat** is worn on the head.
*Un **chapeau** se porte sur la tête.*

## to have    *avoir*

I **have** a book in my hand.
*J'ai un livre à la main.*

I **had** a visitor last week.
*J'ai eu un visiteur la semaine dernière.*

| I have | I shall have | I had |
|--------|--------------|-------|
| *J'ai* | *J'aurai* | *J'ai eu* |

## hay    *foin*

**Hay** is dried grass.
*Le foin est de l'herbe séchée.*

The farmer puts **hay** in a haystack to dry.
*Le fermier entasse le foin en meules pour le faire sécher.*

## he    *il*

Bill is a boy.
*Bill est un garçon.*

**He** is a boy.
*Il est un garçon.*

| he | him | his |
|----|-----|-----|
| *il* | *lui, le* | *son, sa, ses* |

## head
### tête, en *haut de*

1. Tom has turned his **head**.
   *Tom a tourné la tête.*

   The **head** of the pin is green.
   *La tête de l'épingle est verte.*

2. Betty is at the **head** of the stairs.
   *Betty est en haut de l'escalier.*

## health    *santé*

When we are well, we are in good **health**.
*Quand nous allons bien, nous sommes en bonne santé.*

When we are ill, we are in poor **health**.
*Quand nous sommes malades, nous sommes en mauvaise santé.*

## to hear    *entendre*

We **hear** with our ears.
*Nous entendons avec nos oreilles.*

| I hear | I shall hear | I heard |
|--------|--------------|---------|
| *J'entends* | *J'entendrai* | *J'ai entendu* |

## heart    *cœur*

Our **hearts** beat in our bodies.
*Le cœur bat dans notre corps.*

## heat    *chaleur*

Fire gives off **heat**.
*Le feu dégage de la chaleur.*

## heavy    *lourd*

The box is too **heavy** to lift.
*La boîte est trop lourde à soulever.*

## hello    *bonjour*

We say "**Hello**" when we meet someone.
*Quand nous rencontrons quelqu'un, nous lui disons "Bonjour"*

Bill says "**Hello**" to Mary.
*Bill dit "Bonjour" à Marie.*

## to help    *aider*

Ann **helps** Mother with the dishes.
*Anne aide Maman à faire la vaisselle.*

| I help | I shall help | I helped |
|--------|--------------|----------|
| *J'aide* | *J'aiderai* | *J'ai aidé* |

## hen    *poule*

The **hens** are in the chicken run.
*Les poules sont dans le poulailler.*

## her    *son, sa, ses, elle*

1. Those are **her** hat, **her** skirt and **her** shoes.
   *Ce sont son chapeau, sa jupe et ses souliers.*

2. It is for **her**.
   *C'est pour elle.*

# here    *ici*

"Come **here**, Rover", said Tom.
*" Viens **ici**, Rover ," a dit Tim.*

# to hide    *cacher*

We are playing "**hide**-and-seek".
*Nous jouons à **cache-cache**.*

Where did Judy **hide**?
*Où Judy s'est-elle **cachée**?*

| I hide | I shall hide | I hid |
|---|---|---|
| *Je me cache* | *Je me cacherai* | *Je me suis caché* |

# high    *haut*

The kite is **high** in the sky.
*Le cerf-volant est **haut** dans le ciel.*

# hill
## colline

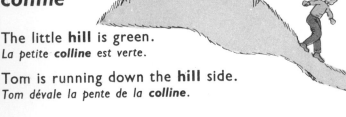

The little **hill** is green.
*La petite **colline** est verte.*

Tom is running down the **hill** side.
*Tom dévale la pente de la **colline**.*

# his    *son, sa, ses*

He had **his** hat, **his** pipe and **his** gloves.
*Il avait **son** chapeau, **sa** pipe et **ses** gants.*

# to hit    *frapper*

John **hit** the ball.
*Jean a **frappé** la balle.*

| I hit | I shall hit | I hit |
|---|---|---|
| *Je frappe* | *Je frapperai* | *J'ai frappé* |

# to hold    *tenir*

Alice **holds** the flower.
*Alice **tient** la fleur.*

| I hold | I shall hold | I held |
|---|---|---|
| *Je tiens* | *Je tiendrai* | *J'ai tenu* |

# hole    *trou*

There is a **hole** in the coat.
*Il y a un **trou** dans la veste.*

# holiday    *jour de fête*    *vacance*

Christmas and Easter are **holidays**.
*Noël et Pâques sont des **jours de fête**.*

# hollow    *creux*

The squirrel lives in a **hollow** tree.
*L'écureuil vit dans un arbre **creux**.*

# home    *maison*

Mother is at **home**.
*Maman est à la **maison**.*

# hook    *crochet, hameçon*

1. I hang my clothes on a **hook**.
   *Je suspends mes vêtements à un **crochet**.*

2. Father catches fish with a fish**hook**.
   *Papa attrape le poisson avec un **hameçon**.*

# hoop    *cerceau*

Tim rolls a **hoop**.
*Tim fait rouler un **cerceau**.*

# to hop
## sauter à cloche-pied

George **hops** on one foot.
*Georges **saute à cloche-pied**.*

| I hop | I shall hop | I hopped |
|---|---|---|
| *Je saute* | *Je sauterai* | *J'ai sauté* |

## horn
### corne, trompette

1. The goat has **horns** on its head.
   *La chèvre a des **cornes** sur la tête.*

2. Peter blows the **horn**.
   *Pierre souffle dans la **trompette**.*

## horse    *cheval*

A **horse** is a big animal.
*Un **cheval** est un gros animal.*

We ride some **horses**.
*Nous montons certains **chevaux**.*

Other **horses** pull carts.
*D'autres **chevaux** tirent des charrettes.*

## hot    *chaud*

In the kettle, the water is **hot**.
*Dans la bouilloire, l'eau est **chaude**.*

## hour    *heure*

**Hours** measure time.
*Les **heures** mesurent le temps.*

There are 24 **hours** in a day.
*Il y a 24 **heures** dans une journée.*

## house    *maison*

A **house** is a building.
*Une **maison** est un bâtiment.*

People live in **houses**.
*Les gens vivent dans des **maisons**.*

## how    *comment*

1. **How** do you make it?
   *Comment le faites-vous ?*

2. How far is it?
   *A quelle distance est-il ?*

3. **How** are you?
   *Comment allez-vous ?*

## how much    *combien*

How much is the bag of flour?
*Combien coûte le paquet de farine ?*

## how many    *combien*

**How many** marbles are there?
*Combien y a-t-il de billes ?*

## to be hungry
### avoir faim

Rover **is hungry**.
*Rover a **faim**.*

I am hungry
*J'ai faim*

I shall be hungry
*J'aurai faim*

I was hungry
*J'ai eu faim*

## to hunt
### chasser

The men are going to **hunt** a fox.
*Les hommes vont **chasser** un renard.*

I hunt
*Je chasse*

I shall hunt
*Je chasserai*

I hunted
*J'ai chassé*

## to hurry    *se dépêcher*

Jack **hurries** to school.
*Jacques **se dépêche** d'aller à l'école.*

I hurry
*Je me dépêche*

I shall hurry
*Je me dépêcherai*

I hurried
*Je me suis dépêché*

## to hurt    *blesser*

Lassie has **hurt** her paw.
*Lassie s'est **blessée** à la patte.*

I hurt
*Je blesse*

I shall hurt
*Je blesserai*

I hurt
*J'ai blessé*

## hut    *cabane*

The boys built a little **hut**.
*Les garçons ont construit une petite **cabane**.*

# I i

Ninth letter of the alphabet.
*Neuvième lettre de l'alphabet.*

## I    *je*

What a good boy am **I** !
*Que **je** suis gentil !*

| I | me | my | mine |
|---|---|---|---|
| *je* | *me, moi* | *mon* | *le mien* |

To whom did it happen? To **me**.
*A qui est-ce arrivé ? A **moi**.*

## ice    *glace*

1. **Ice** is frozen water.
   *La **glace** est de l'eau gelée.*
2. Bill is skating on the **ice**.
   *Bill patine sur la **glace**.*
3. There is **ice** in the refrigerator.
   *Il y a de la **glace** dans le réfrigérateur.*

## ice cream    *glace*

**Ice cream** is good to eat.
*Les **glaces** sont bonnes à manger.*

## if    *si*

**If** it rains, Ruth will put up the umbrella.
*S'il pleut, Ruth ouvrira le parapluie.*

See **if** the door is locked.
*Regardez **si** la porte est fermée.*

## ill    *malade*

Patsy is **ill**.
*Patsy est **malade**.*

## important    *important*

It is **important** to get to school on time.
*Il est **important** d'arriver à l'école à l'heure.*

## in    *dans*

The baby is **in** the pram.
*Le bébé est **dans** la voiture.*

## inch    *pouce*

An **inch** is an English and American measure.
*Le **pouce** est une mesure anglaise et américaine.*

There are twelve **inches** in a foot.
*Il y a douze **pouces** dans un pied.*

## Indian    *Indien*

**Indians** lived in America before the white men came.
*Les **Indiens** vivaient en Amérique avant que les blancs n'arrivent.*

**Indians** still live in America.
*Les **Indiens** vivent encore en Amérique.*

## ink    *encre*

We write with pen and **ink**.
*Nous écrivons avec une plume et de l'encre.*

## insect    *insecte*

**Insects** are very small animals.
*Les **insectes** sont de très petits animaux.*

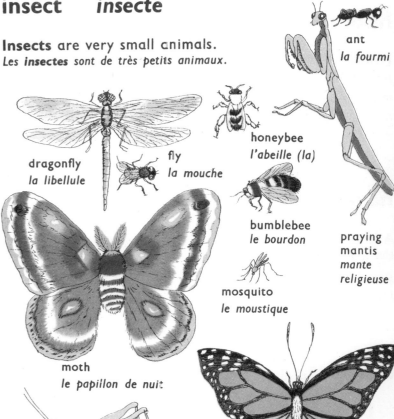

ant
la fourmi

dragonfly
la libellule

fly
la mouche

honeybee
l'abeille (la)

bumblebee
le bourdon

praying mantis
mante religieuse

mosquito
le moustique

moth
le papillon de nuit

grasshopper
la sauterelle

cockroach
la blatte

butterfly
le papillon de jour

These are **insects**.
*Ce sont des **insectes**.*

## inside
### à l'intérieur de

John is **inside** the house.
*Jean est **à l'intérieur de** la maison.*

## instead of  *au lieu de*

May I have milk **instead of** water?
*Puis-je avoir du lait **au lieu d'**eau ?*

## into  *dans*

The rabbit went **into** the hole.
*Le lapin est entré **dans** le trou.*

## iron  *fer*

1. **Iron** is a strong metal.
   *Le **fer** est un métal résistant.*
2. Mother uses an electric **iron**.
   *Maman se sert d'un **fer** électrique.*

## island  *île*

An **island** is land with water all around it.
*Une **île** est une terre entourée d'eau.*

## it  *il*

1. I have a wagon. **It** is red.
   *J'ai un camion. **Il** est rouge.*
2. **It** is fine today.
   ***Il** fait beau aujourd'hui.*

# J j

Tenth letter of the alphabet.
*Dixième lettre de l'alphabet.*

## jacket  *jaquette*

A **jacket** is a short coat.
*Une **jaquette** est un manteau court.*

## jam  *confiture*

**Jam** is made from fruit and sugar.
*La **confiture** est faite de fruits et de sucre.*

We eat **jam** on bread.
*Nous mangeons de la **confiture** sur du pain.*

## jar  *bocal*

We put fruit in glass **jars** to keep it all winter.

*Nous mettons les fruits dans des **bocaux** pour les conserver tout l'hiver.*

## jelly
### gelée

**Jelly** is made from fruit and sugar.
*La **gelée** est faite de fruits et de sucre.*

We eat **jellies** at parties.
*Nous mangeons de la **gelée** aux fêtes.*

## jewel  *bijou*

A **jewel** is a bright and beautiful stone.
*Un **bijou** est une pierre brillante et magnifique.*

## to join
### attacher

**Join** two pieces of string.
***Attachez** deux morceaux de ficelles.*

| I join | I shall join | I joined |
|--------|--------------|----------|
| *J'attache* | *J'attacherai* | *J'ai attach* |

## joke  *plaisanterie*

A **joke** is a funny story.
*Une **plaisanterie** est une histoire comique.*

## joy   *joie*

The dog was happy.
*Le chien était heureux.*

He wagged his tail with **joy**.
*Il remuait la queue de **joie**.*

## juice   *jus*

We squeeze **juice** from fruit.
*Nous extrayons le **jus** des fruits.*

We drink orange **juice**.
*Nous buvons du **jus** d'orange.*

## to jump   *sauter*

Sue likes to **jump** over the rope.
*Suzanne aime **sauter** à la corde.*

| I jump | I shall jump | I jumped |
|---|---|---|
| *Je saute* | *Je sauterai* | *J'ai sauté* |

## just   *juste*

1. We have **just** enough milk to fill the glass.
   *Nous avons **juste** assez de lait pour remplir le verre.*

2. The teacher is **just**.
   *Le professeur est **juste**.*

# K k

Eleventh letter of the alphabet.
*Onzième lettre de l'alphabet.*

## to keep
## *garder*

I **keep** my rabbit in a box.
*Je **garde** mon lapin dans une boîte.*

George gave me a ball.
*Georges m'a donné une balle.*

I may **keep** it.
*Je peux la **garder**.*

| I keep | I shall keep | I kept |
|---|---|---|
| *Je garde* | *Je garderai* | *J'ai gardé* |

## kettle   *bouilloire*

We heat water in a **kettle**.
*Nous chauffons l'eau dans une **bouilloire**.*

## key   *clef*

We lock the door with a **key**.
*Nous fermons la porte avec une **clef**.*

## kick
## *coup de pied*

Ronald gives the ball a **kick**.
*Ronald donne un **coup de pied** à la balle.*

## kindergarten
## *jardin d'enfants*

Little children go to **kindergarten**.
*Les petits enfants vont au **jardin d'enfants**.*

## king
## *roi*

Some countries have a **king**.
*Certains pays ont un **roi**.*

A **king** may wear a crown.
*Un **roi** peut porter une couronne.*

## kiss
## *baiser*

Tom's sister gives him a **kiss**.
*La sœur de Tom lui donne un **baiser**.*

## kitchen
## cuisine

We cook in the **kitchen**.
*Nous faisons la cuisine dans la cuisine.*

## kite  *cerf-volant*

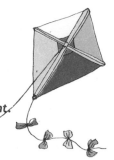

Jim flew his **kite** on a windy day.
*Jim a fait voler son cerf-volant un jour de vent.*

## kitten  *chaton*

A **kitten** is a young cat.
*Un chaton est un jeune chat.*

## knee  *genou*

Our legs bend at the **knee**.
*Nos jambes se plient au genou.*

John sits on his father's **knee**.
*Jean est assis sur les genoux de son père.*

## knife  *couteau*

A **knife** is for cutting.
*Un couteau sert à couper.*

We put **knives** and forks on the table.
*Nous disposons des couteaux et des fourchettes sur la table.*

## to knock  *frapper*

1. Ann **knocks** at the door.
   *Anne frappe à la porte.*
2. She **knocks** with the knocker.
   *Elle frappe avec le heurtoir.*

| I knock | I shall knock | I knocked |
|---|---|---|
| Je frappe | Je frapperai | J'ai frappé |

## knot  *nœud*

I tied a **knot** in the rope.
*J'ai fait un nœud à la corde.*

## to know  *savoir, connaître*

1. Do you **know** where Paris is?
   *Savez-vous où est Paris?*
2. Do you **know** Paris?
   *Connaissez-vous Paris?*

| I know | I shall know | I knew |
|---|---|---|
| Je sais | Je saurai | J'ai su |
| Je connais | Je connaîtrai | J'ai connu |

# L l

Twelfth letter of the alphabet.
*Douzième lettre de l'alphabet.*

## lace
## dentelle
## lacet
## to lace  *lacer*

1. We use **lace** for trimming dresses.
   *Nous utilisons la dentelle pour garnir les robes.*
2. Peter **laces** his shoe with a **lace**.
   *Pierre lace son soulier avec un lacet.*

| I lace | I shall lace | I laced |
|---|---|---|
| Je lace | Je lacerai | J'ai lacé |

## ladder
## échelle

We use a **ladder** for climbing.
*Nous utilisons une échelle pour grimper.*

## lake
## lac

A **lake** is a large body of water surrounded by land.
*Un lac est une vaste étendue d'eau entourée de terre.*

# lamp *lampe*

A **lamp** gives us light.
*La lampe nous donne de la lumière.*

# land terre
# to land *atterrir*

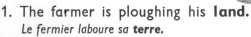

1. The farmer is ploughing his **land.**
   *Le fermier laboure sa terre.*
2. Joe jumped from the wall.
   *Joe a sauté du mur.*

   He **landed** on the grass.
   *Il a atterri sur l'herbe.*

| I land | I shall land | I landed |
|---|---|---|
| *J'atterris* | *J'atterrirai* | *J'ai atterri* |

# large *grand*

An eagle is a **large** bird.
*L'aigle est un grand oiseau.*

# last *dernier*
# to last *durer*

1. John is the **last** to jump.
   *Jean est le dernier à sauter.*
2. How long will the rain **last?**
   *Combien de temps la pluie durera-t-elle ?*

| It lasts | It will last | It lasted |
|---|---|---|
| *Cela dure* | *Cela durera* | *Cela a duré* |

# late
# en retard, tard

1. Peter is **late** for breakfast.
   *Pierre est en retard pour le petit déjeuner.*
2. It was **late** in the evening.
   *C'était tard dans la soirée.*

# to laugh *rire*

Funny things make us **laugh.**
*Les choses amusantes nous font rire.*

We **laugh** when we are happy.
*Nous rions quand nous sommes heureux.*

| I laugh | I shall laugh | I laughed |
|---|---|---|
| *Je ris* | *Je rirai* | *J'ai ri* |

# lawn *pelouse*

Grass grows on our **lawn.**
*L'herbe pousse sur notre pelouse.*

# to lay
# poser, pondre

1. Ruth **lays** her doll in the cradle.
   *Ruth pose sa poupée dans le berceau.*
2. The hen has **laid** an egg.
   *La poule a pondu un œuf.*

| I lay | I shall lay | I laid |
|---|---|---|
| *Je pose* | *Je poserai* | *J'ai posé* |

# to lead *conduire*
# leader *chef*

1. The man **leads** the horse.
   *L'homme conduit le cheval.*
2. Jim is the **leader** of the file.
   *Jim est le chef de file.*

| I lead | I shall lead | I led |
|---|---|---|
| *Je conduis* | *Je conduirai* | *J'ai conduit* |

# leaf *feuille*

A **leaf** is green.
*Une feuille est verte.*

**Leaves** grow on trees and plants.
*Les feuilles poussent sur les arbres et les plantes.*

# to learn *apprendre*

Susie will **learn** how to sew.
*Suzanne apprendra à coudre.*

| I learn | I shall learn | I learned |
|---|---|---|
| *J'apprends* | *J'apprendrai* | *J'ai appris* |

# to leave *laisser, quitter*

1. Children **leave** their stockings by the chimney for Father Christmas.

   *Les enfants laissent leurs bas près de la cheminée pour le Père Noël.*

2. Mother **left** the house.
   *Maman a quitté la maison.*

| I leave | I shall leave | I left |
|---|---|---|
| *Je laisse* | *Je laisserai* | *J'ai laissé* |
| *Je quitte* | *Je quitterai* | *J'ai quitté* |

51

## left    *gauche*

I have two hands.
*J'ai deux mains.*

One is my **left** hand.
*L'une est ma main gauche.*

The other is my right hand.
*L'autre est ma main droite.*

## leg    *jambe, pied*

1. We stand on our **legs**.
   *Nous nous tenons sur nos jambes.*
2. Chairs have **legs**.
   *Les chaises ont des pieds.*

## length    *longueur*

What is the **length** of the plank?
*Quelle est la longueur de la planche ?*

It is ninety centimetres long.
*Sa longueur est de quatre-vingt-dix centimètres.*

## less    *moins*

If I take one of your pears,
you will have one pear **less**.
*Si je prends une de vos poires,
vous aurez une poire de moins.*

## to let    *laisser*

We **let** the bird out of the cage.
*Nous laissons l'oiseau hors de la cage.*

Will you **let** me use your pencil?
*Voulez-vous me laisser utiliser votre crayon ?*

| I let | I shall let | I let |
|---|---|---|
| *Je laisse* | *Je laisserai* | *J'ai laissé* |

## letter    *lettre*

There are 26 **letters** in
the English alphabet.
*Il y a 26 lettres dans l'alphabet anglais.*

L is a **letter**.
*L est une lettre.*

The **letter** came by post.
*La lettre est arrivée par la poste.*

## library    *bibliothèque*

Books are kept in a **library**.
*Les livres sont rangés dans une bibliothèque.*

## lid    *couvercle*

We cover some things with **lids**.
*Nous couvrons certains objets avec un couvercle.*

## lie    *mensonge*
## to lie    *mentir, être couché*

1. Harry did not tell the truth.
   He told a **lie**.
   *Henri n'a pas dit la vérité.
   Il a dit un mensonge.*
2. Why did he **lie**?
   *Pourquoi a-t-il menti ?*
3. I **lie** in my bed and sleep.
   *Je suis couché dans mon lit et je dors.*

| I lie | I shall lie | I lied |
|---|---|---|
| *Je mens* | *Je mentirai* | *J'ai menti* |

| I lie | I shall lie | I lay |
|---|---|---|
| *Je me couche* | *Je me coucherai* | *Je me suis couché* |

## to lift    *soulever*

The man will **lift** the ice.
*L'homme soulèvera la glace.*

| I lift | I shall lift | I lifted |
|---|---|---|
| *Je soulève* | *Je soulèverai* | *J'ai soulevé* |

## light
## *lumière, clair, léger*

1. The sun gives **light**.
   *Le soleil donne de la lumière.*
2. Ann's dress is a **light** colour.
   *La robe d'Anne est d'une couleur claire.*
3. The balloon is **light**.
   *Le ballon est léger.*

## like    *pareil, comme*
## to like    *aimer*

1. My cat is **like** your cat.
   *Mon chat est pareil à votre chat.*
2. **Like** you, I **like** cats.
   *Comme vous, j'aime les chats.*

| I like | I shall like | I liked |
|---|---|---|
| *J'aime* | *J'aimerai* | *J'ai aimé* |

## line  corde
## rang, ligne

1. The clothes are on the clothes**line**.
   *Les vêtements sont sur la **corde** à linge.*

2. The children wait in **line**.
   *Les enfants attendent en **rang**.*

3. John drew a red **line**.
   *Jean a dessiné une **ligne** rouge.*

## lip  *lèvre*

We have two **lips**.
*Nous avons deux **lèvres**.*

We speak with our **lips**.
*Nous parlons avec nos **lèvres**.*

## liquid  *liquide*

Water is **liquid**.
*L'eau est **liquide**.*

There are many **liquids**.
*Il y a beaucoup de **liquides**.*

We can pour **liquids**.
*Nous pouvons verser les **liquides**.*

## little  *petit*

A mouse is a **little** animal.
*La souris est un **petit** animal.*

## to live  *vivre*

The goldfish **live** in a bowl.
*Les poissons rouges **vivent** dans un bocal.*

| I live | I shall live | I lived |
|---|---|---|
| *Je vis* | *Je vivrai* | *J'ai vécu* |

## long  *long*

John's sweater is **long**.
*Le chandail de Jean est **long**.*

The kite string is very **long**.
*La corde du cerf-volant est très **longue**.*

## to look  *regarder*

**Look** at the aeroplane.
*Regardez l'avion.*

| I look | I shall look | I looked |
|---|---|---|
| *Je regarde* | *Je regarderai* | *J'ai regardé* |

## to look for
## chercher

I am **looking for** my hat.
*Je **cherche** mon chapeau.*

| I look for | I shall look for |
|---|---|
| *Je cherche* | *Je chercherai* |
| I looked for | |
| *J'ai cherché* | |

## to lose  *perdre*

Do not **lose** your mittens
*Ne **perdez** pas vos moufles.*

I am **lost**.
*Je suis **perdu**.*

| I lose | I shall lose | I lost |
|---|---|---|
| *Je perds* | *Je perdrai* | *J'ai perdu* |

## loud  *fort*

The lion gave a **loud** roar.
*Le lion poussa un **fort** rugissement.*

## to love  *aimer*

I **love** my dog.
*J'**aime** mon chien.*

| I love | I shall love | I loved |
|---|---|---|
| *J'aime* | *J'aimerai* | *J'ai aimé* |

## low  *bas*

The bookshelves are **low**.
*Les étagères à livres sont **basses**.*

## lunch  *déjeuner*
## to lunch  *déjeuner*

1. **Lunch** is a light meal.
   *Le **déjeuner** est un léger repas.*

2. I **lunch** at noon.
   *Je **déjeune** à midi.*

| I lunch | I shall lunch | I lunched |
|---|---|---|
| *Je déjeune* | *Je déjeunerai* | *J'ai déjeuné* |

# M m

## machine   *machine*

**Machines** do work.
*Les machines font le travail.*

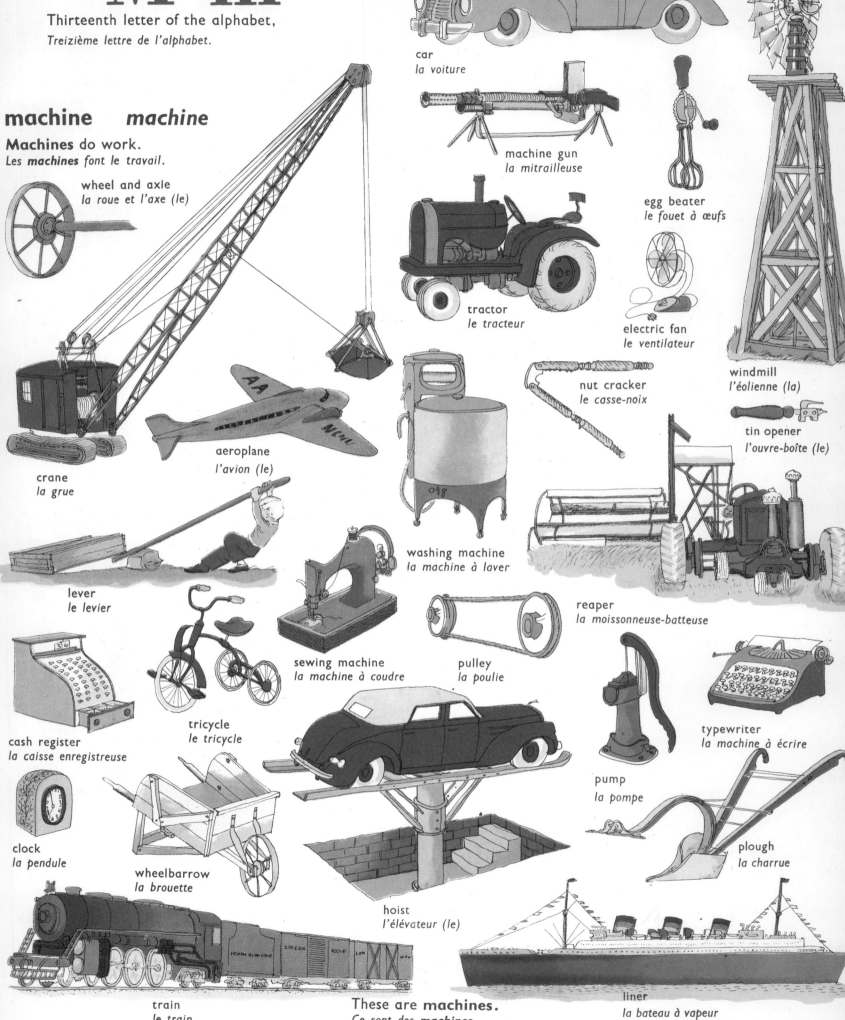

wheel and axle
*la roue et l'axe (le)*

crane
*la grue*

lever
*le levier*

aeroplane
*l'avion (le)*

cash register
*la caisse enregistreuse*

clock
*la pendule*

tricycle
*le tricycle*

sewing machine
*la machine à coudre*

wheelbarrow
*la brouette*

train
*le train*

car
*la voiture*

machine gun
*la mitrailleuse*

tractor
*le tracteur*

washing machine
*la machine à laver*

hoist
*l'élévateur (le)*

pulley
*la poulie*

These are **machines.**
*Ce sont des machines.*

egg beater
*le fouet à œufs*

electric fan
*le ventilateur*

nut cracker
*le casse-noix*

reaper
*la moissonneuse-batteuse*

pump
*la pompe*

typewriter
*la machine à écrire*

plough
*la charrue*

liner
*la bateau à vapeur*

windmill
*l'éolienne (la)*

tin opener
*l'ouvre-boîte (le)*

54

# to make    *faire*

Mother will **make** a cake.
*Maman **fera** un gâteau.*

The bell **makes** a noise.
*La cloche **fait** du bruit.*

Two and two **make** four.
*Deux et deux **font** quatre.*

| I make | I shall make | I made |
|--------|--------------|--------|
| *Je fais* | *Je ferai* | *J'ai fait* |

# man    *homme*

Father is a **man**.
*Papa est un **homme**.*

These are **men**.
*Voici des **hommes**.*

# many    *beaucoup*
# how many
# combien

**How many** marbles have you?
***Combien** avez-vous de billes?*

I have **many** marbles.
*J'ai **beaucoup** de billes.*

# to march
# marcher

The school children **march** in line.
*Les écoliers **marchent** en rang.*

| I march | I shall march | I marched |
|---------|---------------|-----------|
| *Je marche* | *Je marcherai* | *J'ai marché* |

# mark    *signe*

Lucy put a **mark** on the board.
*Lucie a fait un **signe** sur le tableau.*

# market    *marché*

We go to the **market** to buy things.
*Nous allons au **marché** pour faire des achats.*

# match    *allumette*

We use a **match** to light a fire.
*Nous employons une **allumette** pour allumer un feu.*

# me    *moi, me*

1. He gave **me** a book.
   *Il **m'a** donné un livre.*

2. He gave it to **me**.
   *Il **me** l'a donné.*

3. It is for **me**.
   *C'est pour **moi**.*

# meal    *repas*

We have three **meals** a day.
*Nous prenons trois **repas** par jour.*

We eat and drink at **meal**time.
*Nous mangeons et buvons pendant les **repas***

Dinner is a **meal**.
*Le dîner est un **repas**.*

# measure    *mesure*
# to measure    *mesurer*

1. An inch is a **measure** of length.
   *Un pouce est une **mesure** de longueur.*

2. We will **measure** the ribbon to see how long it is.
   *Nous **mesurerons** le ruban pour savoir sa longueur.*

| I measure | I shall measure | I measured |
|-----------|-----------------|------------|
| *Je mesure* | *Je mesurerai* | *J'ai mesuré* |

# meat    *viande*

We eat **meat**.                chicken    roast    chop
*Nous mangeons de la **viande**.* poulet    rôti    côtelette

The butcher sells us **meat**.
*Le boucher nous vend de la **viande**.*    sausages
                                            saucisses

## medicine
### médecine, médicaments

1. **Medicine** helps to make us well.
   *La **médecine** nous aide à guérir.*

2. We take **medicine** when we are ill.
   *Nous prenons des **médicaments** quand nous sommes malades.*

## to meet     rencontrer

Bill runs to **meet** his father.
*Bill court pour **rencontrer** son père.*

| I meet | I shall meet | I met |
|---|---|---|
| *Je rencontre* | *Je rencontrerai* | *J'ai rencontré* |

## to melt    fondre

The snowman **melts** in the sun.
*Le bonhomme de neige **fond** au soleil.*

| I melt | I shall melt | I melted |
|---|---|---|
| *Je fonds* | *Je fondrai* | *J'ai fondu* |

## metal
### métal

**Metal** is found in the ground.
*Le **métal** se trouve dans le sol.*

Goid and iron are **metals**.
*L'or et le fer sont des **métaux**.*

These things are made of **metal**.
*Ces objets sont en **métal**.*

## middle    milieu

Jane sits in the **middle** of the bench.
*Jeanne est assise au **milieu** du banc.*

The hole is in the **middle** of the biscuit.
*Le trou est au **milieu** du biscuit.*

## mile    mille

A **mile** is a measure of distance.
*Un **mille** est une mesure de distance.*

It takes about twenty minutes to walk a **mile**.
*Il faut environ vingt minutes pour franchir un **mille** à pied.*

## milk    lait

Cows give us **milk**.
*Les vaches nous donnent du **lait**.*

The milkman brings the **milk**.
*Le laitier apporte le **lait**.*

## mill    moulin, usine

Many things are made in **mills**.
*Beaucoup de choses se font dans les **usines**.*

Flour is ground in a **mill**.
*La farine se moud dans un **moulin**.*

A **windmill** is turned by the wind.
*Un **moulin-à-vent** est actionné par le vent.*

The miller grinds the flour.
*Le meunier moud la farine.*

## mind    esprit

Thoughts are formed in our **minds**.
*Les pensées se forment dans notre **esprit**.*

## mine    le mien, la mienne

Whose skirt is it?
*A qui est la jupe ?*

It's **mine**.
*C'est la **mienne**.*

## mine    mine

Coal is dug in **mines**.
*Le charbon est extrait dans les **mines**.*

## minute    minute

A **minute** is a measure of time.
*Une **minute** est une mesure de temps.*

## miss
### manquer

We **missed** the train.
*Nous avons **manqué** le train.*

| I miss | I shall miss | I missed |
|---|---|---|
| *Je manque* | *Je manquerai* | *J'ai manqué* |

## mistake    *erreur*

A **mistake** is something wrong.
*Une **erreur** est quelque chose d'inexact.*

Tom said two and two make five.
*Tom disait que deux et deux font cinq.*

Tom made a **mistake**.
*Tom faisait une **erreur**.*

## mitten    *moufle*

We wear **mittens** on our hands to keep them warm.

*Nous portons des **moufles** aux mains pour les tenir au chaud.*

## to mix    *mélanger*

1. The alphabet bricks are **mixed up**.
   *Les cubes alphabétiques sont **mélangés**.*

2. Sue and Ted **mix** sand and water to make mud pies.

   *Suzon et Ted **mélangent** le sable à l'eau pour faire des pâtés.*

| I mix | I shall mix | I mixed |
|---|---|---|
| *Je mélange* | *Je mélangerai* | *J'ai mélangé* |

## money    *argent*

We use **money** to buy things.
*Nous employons de l'**argent** pour faire les achats.*

## monkey    *singe*

**Monkeys** are animals.
*Les **singes** sont des animaux.*

They climb trees.
*Ils grimpent aux arbres.*

## month    *mois*

A **month** is a measure of time.
*Le **mois** est une mesure de temps.*

There are 12 **months** in a year.
*Il y a 12 **mois** dans une année.*

They are January, February, March, April, May, June, July, August, September, October, November and December.

*Ce sont janvier, février, mars, avril, mai, juin, juillet, août, septembre, octobre, novembre et décembre.*

## moon    *lune*

We see the **moon** at night.
*Nous voyons la **lune** la nuit.*

## more
### encore,    plus de

1. Will you have some **more** soup?
   *Voulez-vous **encore** du potage?*

2. John has **more** pencils than Jane.
   *Jean a **plus de** crayons que Jeanne.*

## morning    *matin, matinée*

1. We get up in the **morning**.
   *Nous nous levons le **matin**.*

2. **Morning** is the first part of the day.
   *La **matinée** est la première partie de la journée.*

## most    *le plus de*

Alice has more ice cream than Bruce
*Alice a plus de glace que Bruce.*

John has the **most** ice cream.
*C'est Jean qui a **le plus de** glace.*

## mother    *mère, maman*

1. The **mother** loves her baby.
   *La **mère** aime son bébé.*

   I live with my father and **mother**.
   *J'habite avec mon père et ma **mère**.*

2. I love **Mother**.
   *J'aime **maman**.*

## mountain
### montagne

The **mountain** is higher than the hills.
*La **montagne** est plus haute que les collines.*

## mouse    *souris*

A **mouse** is a small animal.
*La **souris** est un petit animal.*

**Mice** like cheese.
*Les **souris** aiment le fromage.*

## mouth   *bouche*

Peter has his **mouth** open.
*Pierre a la **bouche** ouverte.*

We eat and talk with our **mouths**.
*Nous mangeons et parlons avec notre **bouche**.*

## to move   *remuer   déménager*

1. I **move** my legs when I run.
   *Je **remue** les jambes quand je cours.*
2. We **moved** to a new town last week.
   *Nous avons **déménagé** dans une nouvelle ville la semaine dernière.*

| I move | I shall move | I moved |
|---|---|---|
| Je remue | Je remuerai | J'ai remué |
| je déménage | Je déménagerai | J'ai déménagé |

## much   *beaucoup*

Is there **much** sugar ?
*Y a-t-il **beaucoup** de sucre ?*

I have **much** work to do.
*J'ai **beaucoup** de travail à faire.*

## mud   *boue*

**Mud** is wet earth.
*La **boue** est de la terre mouillée.*

The rain makes the road **muddy.**
*La pluie rend la route **boueuse.***

## music   *musique*

We like to hear **music.**
*Nous aimons entendre de la **musique.***

We sing and dance to **music.**
*Nous chantons et dansons au son de la **musique.***

This is written **music.**
*Ceci est de la **musique** écrite.*

## my   *mon, ma, mes*

Mother gave me **my** hat, **my** dress and **my** shoes.
*Maman m'a donné **mon** chapeau, **ma** robe et **mes** souliers.*

# N n

Fourteenth letter of the alphabet.
*Quatorzième lettre de l'alphabet.*

## nail
## *clou*
## *ongle*

1. We join wood with **nails.**
   *Nous assemblons le bois avec des **clous.***

   John drives a **nail** into the plank.
   *Jean enfonce un **clou** dans la planche.*

2. We have **nails** at the ends of our fingers and toes.
   *Nous avons des **ongles** à l'extrémité de nos doigts et de nos orteils.*

## name   *nom*

We call each other by our **names.**
*Nous nous appelons par nos **noms.***

We know the **names** of many things.
*Nous savons le **nom** de beaucoup de choses.*

## narrow   *étroit*

The space is too **narrow** for the pig to go through.

*L'ouverture est trop **étroite** pour que le cochon la franchisse.*

## near   *près*

The dogs are **near** us.
*Les chiens sont **près** de nous.*

## neat   *en ordre*

Mary keeps her desk **neat.**
*Marie garde son bureau **en ordre.***

## neck    cou, col

1. Father wears a tie around his **neck**.
   *Père porte une cravate autour de son* **cou**.

   Swans have long **necks**.
   *Les cygnes ont de longs* **cous**.

2. Bottles have narrow **necks**.
   *Les bouteilles ont des* **cols** *étroits*.

## to need    avoir besoin de

We **need** air to breathe.
*Nous* **avons besoin d'***air pour respirer*.

| I need | I shall need | I needed |
|---|---|---|
| *J'ai besoin* | *J'aurai besoin* | *J'ai eu besoin* |

## needle    aiguille

Jane sews with a **needle**.
*Jeanne coud avec une* **aiguille**.

## neighbour    voisin

A **neighbour** is someone who lives near you.
*Un* **voisin** *est quelqu'un qui habite près de vous*.

## nest    nid

Birds build **nests**.
*Les oiseaux construisent des* **nids**.

They lay eggs and bring up their young in **nests**.
*Ils pondent des œufs et élèvent leurs petits dans des* **nids**.

## net    filet

Ruth has a **net** on her hair.
*Ruth a un* **filet** *sur les cheveux*.

The fisherman catches fish in his **net**.
*Le pêcheur prend le poisson dans son* **filet**.

## never    ne......jamais

I am six years old.
*J'ai six ans*.

I shall **never** be five again.
*Je n'aurai plus* **jamais** *cinq ans*.

He **never** came.
*Il n'est* **jamais** *venu*.

## new    nouveau, neuf

1. We have a **new** baby brother.
   *Nous avons un* **nouveau** *petit frère*.

2. Donald has **new** shoes.
   *Donald a des souliers* **neufs**.

## news    nouvelles

What is the **news** today?
*Quelles sont les* **nouvelles** *aujourd'hui?*

## newspaper    journal

We read news in the **newspapers**.
*Nous lisons les nouvelles dans les* **journaux**.

## next    prochain, suivant

1. **Next** month, **next** week.
   *Le mois* **prochain**, *la semaine* **prochaine**.

2. Whose turn is **next**?
   *A qui est le tour* **suivant**?

## nice    joli, agréable, gentil

1. We like **nice** things.
   *Nous aimons les* **jolies** *choses*.

2. New clothes are **nice** to wear.
   *Les vêtements neufs sont* **agréables** *à porter*.

3. **Nice** children behave well.
   *Les* **gentils** *enfants se conduisent bien*.

## niece    nièce

Mary is my **niece**. I am Mary's uncle.
*Marie est ma* **nièce**. *Je suis l'oncle de Marie*.

## night    nuit

**Night** comes after the sun sets.
*La* **nuit** *vient après le coucher du soleil*.

It is dark at **night**.
*Il fait sombre la* **nuit**.

## nine    *neuf*

**Nine** is a number.
*Neuf est un nombre.*

Here are **nine** bricks.
*Voici neuf cubes.*

## no    *non, ne......pas de*

1. Do you know the answer?
   *Connaissez-vous la réponse?*

   **No**, I do not know the answer.
   *Non, je ne connais pas la réponse.*

2. There is **no** soup for dinner.
   *Il n'y a pas de potage au dîner.*

## noise    *bruit*

We hear a **noise**.
*Nous entendons du bruit.*

The fire engine made a lot
of **noise**.
*La voiture des pompiers faisait
beaucoup de bruit.*

## none    *aucun*

Are there any eggs in the nest?
*Y a-t-il des œufs dans le nid?*

No. There are **none**.
*Non. Il n'y en a aucun.*

## noon    *midi*

We eat lunch at **noon**.
*Nous déjeunons à midi.*

## north    *nord*

**North** is a direction.
*Le nord est une direction.*

It is very cold at the **North** Pole.
*Il fait très froid au pôle nord.*

## nose    *nez*

I breathe through my **nose**.
*Je respire par le nez.*

I smell with my **nose**.
*Je sens avec mon nez.*

## not    *ne......pas*

Does Bruce go to school?
*Bruce va-t-il à l'école?*

No. Bruce does **not** go to school.
*Non. Bruce ne va pas à l'école.*

## note    *mot, note*

1. Mother wrote a **note**.
   *Maman a écrit un mot.*

2. I will make a **note** of this.
   *Je prendrai note de ceci.*

## nothing    *rien*

There is **nothing** on the plate.
*Il n'y a rien sur l'assiette.*

## now    *maintenant*

You must go to bed **now**.
*Vous devez aller au lit maintenant.*

## number    *nombre, numéro*

1. A **number** shows how many or how much.
   *Le nombre indique la quantité.*

2. We live at **number** 4, Park Street.
   *Nous habitons au numéro 4, rue du Parc.*

## nurse    *infirmière*

A **nurse** looks after invalids.
*Une infirmière soigne les malades.*

## nut    *noix, écrou*

1. **Nuts** grow on trees.
   *Les noix poussent sur les arbres.*

   They have hard shells.
   *Elles ont des coques dures.*

2. We use metal **nuts** in machines.
   *Nous utilisons des écrous de métal dans les
   machines.*

# O o

Fifteenth letter of the alphabet.
*Quinzième lettre de l'alphabet.*

## oak    *chêne*

We have an **oak** in our garden.
*Nous avons un **chêne** dans notre jardin.*

**Oak** is a beautiful wood.
*Le **chêne** est un beau bois.*

## oat
## *avoine*

The farmer grows **oats**.
*Le fermier fait pousser de l'**avoine**.*

## to obey    *obéir*

The dog **obeys** his master.
*Le chien **obéit** à son maître.*

| I obey | I shall obey | I obeyed |
|--------|--------------|----------|
| *J'obéis* | *J'obéirai* | *J'ai obéi* |

## ocean
## *océan*

The **ocean** is filled with salt water
*L'**océan** est rempli d'eau salée.*

The **ocean** covers most of the earth's surface.
*L'**océan** couvre la plus grande partie de la surface de la terre.*

Have you seen the **ocean**?
*Avez-vous vu l'**océan**?*

## of    *de*

He took a piece **of** cake.
*Il prit un morceau **de** gâteau.*

The box is full **of** sweets.
*La boîte est pleine **de** bonbons.*

He gave a smile **of** joy.
*Il sourit **de** joie.*

Bill is a boy **of** six years.
*Bill est un garçon **de** six ans.*

## of the    *du, de la, des*

1. The nose **of the** dog is cold.
   *Le nez **du** chien est froid.*

2. The cover **of the** box is red.
   *Le couvercle **de la** boîte est rouge.*

3. The ears **of the** rabbits are long.
   *Les oreilles **des** lapins sont longues.*

## office    *bureau*

People work in **offices**.
*Les gens travaillent dans des **bureaux**.*

## often    *souvent*

We **often** have ice cream.
*Nous avons **souvent** de la glace.*

## oh    *oh*

We say "**Oh!**" when we are surprised.
*Nous disons "**oh!**" quand nous sommes surpris.*

## oil
## *huile, pétrole*

1. **Oil** is thick liquid.
   *L'**huile** est un liquide épais.*

   We use **oil** in machines.
   *Nous utilisons de l'**huile** dans les machines.*

2. **Oil** is found in the ground.
   *Le **pétrole** se trouve dans le sol.*

## old    *vieux, âgé de*

1. The **old** man can hardly walk.
   *Le **vieil** homme peut à peine marcher.*

   When he was young he could run.
   *Quand il était jeune il pouvait courir.*

   The **old** shoe is of no use.
   *Le **vieux** soulier ne sert plus à rien.*

2. Jim is six years **old**.
   *Jim est **âgé de** six ans.*

## on  *sur*

The flowers are **on** the table.
*Les fleurs sont **sur** la table.*

## once
## *une fois*

**Once** I flew in an aeroplane.
***Une fois** j'ai volé en avion.*

**Once upon a time** there was a princess.
*Il était **une fois** une princesse.*

## one  *un, on*

1. **One** is a number.
   *Un est un nombre.*

   Here is **one** lamb.
   *Voici **un** agneau.*

2. **One** should eat every day.
   ***On** doit manger chaque jour.*

## onion  *oignon*

**Onions** are vegetables.
*Les **oignons** sont des légumes.*

They are good to eat.
*Ils sont bons à manger.*

## only  *seulement*

I have **only** one doll.
*J'ai **seulement** une poupée.*

I wish I had more dolls.
*Je voudrais avoir plus de poupées.*

## open  *ouvert*
## to open  *ouvrir*

1. John **opens** the door.
   *Jean **ouvre** la porte.*

2. It is **open**.
   *Elle est **ouverte**.*

| I open | I shall open | I opened |
| --- | --- | --- |
| J'ouvre | J'ouvrirai | J'ai ouvert |

## or  *ou*

Shall we go by bus **or** by train?
*Irons-nous en autocar **ou** par le train ?*

## orange  *orange*

An orange is a **round** fruit.
*L'**orange** est un fruit rond.*

**Orange** is a colour.
*L'**orange** est une couleur.*

## order  *ordre*
## to order  *commander*

1. Everything is in **order**.
   *Tout est en **ordre**.*

   The captain gave the men an **order**.
   *Le capitaine a donné un **ordre** aux hommes.*

2. Mother **ordered** groceries.
   *Maman a **commandé** de l'épicerie.*

| I order | I shall order | I ordered |
| --- | --- | --- |
| Je commande | Je commanderai | J'ai commandé |

## organ  *orgue*

We hear **organ** music in church.
*Nous entendons la musique de l'**orgue** à l'église.*

## other  *autre*

One of those men is tall.
*Un de ces hommes est grand.*

The **other** man is short.
*L'**autre** homme est petit.*

## out  *hors de, dehors*

1. The mouse came **out** of his hole.
   *La souris sortit **hors de** son trou.*

2. Mother is **out**.
   *Maman est **dehors**.*

## outside
### en dehors de, à l'extérieur

The bird is **outside** the nest.
*L'oiseau est **en dehors de** son nid.*

We play **outside** in warm weather.
*Nous jouons **à l'extérieur** par temps chaud.*

## oven   *four*

Mother bakes a pie in the **oven**.
*Maman fait cuire une tarte dans le **four**.*

## over
### au-dessus de

The aeroplane flew **over** the mountain.
*L'avion volait **au-dessus de** la montagne.*

## owl   *hibou*

An **owl** is a big bird.
*Le **hibou** est un gros oiseau.*

**Owls** hunt at night.
*Les **hiboux** chassent la nuit.*

## to own   *posséder*

I have a rabbit.
*J'ai un lapin.*

I **own** him.
*Je le **possède**.*

I am his owner.
*Je suis son propriétaire.*

| I own | I shall own | I owned |
|---|---|---|
| *Je possède* | *Je posséderai* | *J'ai possédé* |

## ox   *bœuf*

An **ox** looks like a cow.
*Un **bœuf** ressemble à une vache.*

It pulls heavy wagons.
*Il tire de lourds chariots.*

# P p

Sixteenth letter of the alphabet.
*Seizième lettre de l'alphabet.*

## to pack   *emballer*

Jim is **packing** his shirt in his suitcase.
*Jim **emballe** sa chemise dans sa valise.*

| I pack | I shall pack | I packed |
|---|---|---|
| *J'emballe* | *J'emballerai* | *J'ai emballé* |

## package  *paquet*

Ann wrapped up a **package**.
*Anne a enveloppé un **paquet**.*

## page   *page*

Books have many **pages**.
*Les livres ont de nombreuses **pages**.*

## pail   *seau*

Helen fills her **pail** with water.
*Hélène remplit son **seau** avec de l'eau.*

## pain   *mal, douleur*

I have a bad tooth.
*J'ai une dent abîmée.*

1. It gives me **pain**.
   *Elle me fait **mal**.*

2. It is **painful**.
   *C'est **douloureux**.*

## paint
### *peinture*
### *couleurs*
### to paint    *peindre*

1. We colour things with **paint**.
   *Nous colorions les objets avec de la **peinture**.*

2. We **paint** pictures with **paints**.
   *Nous **peignons** des tableaux avec des **couleurs**.*

3. The **painter** is **painting** the door red.
   *Le **peintre** **peint** la porte en rouge.*

| I paint | I shall paint | I painted |
|---------|---------------|-----------|
| *Je peins* | *Je peindrai* | *J'ai peint* |

## pair    *paire*

a pair of shoes
*une paire de souliers*

Two things which are alike make a **pair**.
*Deux choses de même espèce forment une **paire**.*

## pajamas (or pyjamas)    *pyjama*

Peter is wearing **pyjamas**.
*Pierre porte un **pyjama**.*

He is ready for bed.
*Il est prêt à se coucher.*

## palace    *palais*

A **palace** is the home of a king.
*Un **palais** est la maison d'un roi.*

## pan    *casserole*

We cook food in **pans**.
*Nous faisons cuire la nourriture dans des **casseroles**.*

## pancake    *crêpe*

**Pancakes** are food.
*Les **crêpes** sont un aliment.*

**Pancakes** are good with butter.
*Les **crêpes** sont bonnes avec du beurre.*

## paper
### *papier*
### *journal*

1. The pages of this book are **paper**.
   *Les pages de ce livre sont en **papier**.*

2. Father sat reading his **paper**.
   *Papa était assis en train de lire son **journal**.*

## parachute    *parachute*

The **parachute** brings the flier safely down.

*Le **parachute** conduit l'aviateur à terre en sécurité.*

## parade
### *parade*

The circus **parade** goes along the street.
*La **parade** du cirque parcourt la rue.*

## park    *parc*
### to park    *parquer*

1. Mother took Bruce to the **park**.
   *Maman a conduit Bruce au **parc**.*

   Trees and grass grow in the **park**.
   *Des arbres et de l'herbe poussent dans le **parc**.*

2. The car is **parked** in the street.
   *La voiture est **parquée** dans la rue.*

| I park | I shall park | I parked |
|--------|--------------|----------|
| *Je parque* | *Je parquerai* | *J'ai parqué* |

## part    *partie*

Bill ate **part** of the cake.
*Bill a mangé une **partie** du gâteau.*

## party
### *fête*

The children played games at the **party**.
*Les enfants jouèrent à la **fête**.*

## to pass
### dépasser, passer

1. The train will **pass** the car.
   *Le train va **dépasser** l'auto.*

2. **Pass** me the cheese, please.
   ***Passez**-moi le fromage s'il vous plaît.*

| I pass | I will pass | I passed |
|---|---|---|
| *Je dépasse* | *Je dépasserai* | *J'ai dépassé* |
| *Je passe* | *Je passerai* | *J'ai passé* |

## past   *passé, devant*

1. In the **past** you were a baby.
   *Dans le **passé** vous étiez un bébé.*

2. The car went **past** the gate.
   *La voiture passa **devant** le portail.*

## paste   *colle*

**Paste** is used
for sticking things together.
*La **colle** sert à coller les choses ensemble.*

## to pat   *caresser*

John **pats** Rover on the head.
*Jean **caresse** Rover sur la tête.*

He **pats** him softly with his hand.
*Il le **caresse** doucement avec la main.*

| I pat | I shall pat | I patted |
|---|---|---|
| *Je caresse* | *Je caresserai* | *J'ai caressé* |

## patch
### pièce (d'étoffe)

Mother sewed a **patch** over the hole.
*Maman a cousu une **pièce** sur le trou.*

## path   *sentier*

The **path** leads to the gate.
*Le **sentier** conduit au portail.*

## to pay
### payer

Jim's father **pays** for his
newspaper.
*Le père de Jim **paie** son journal.*

| I pay | I shall pay | I paid |
|---|---|---|
| *Je paie* | *Je paierai* | *J'ai payé* |

## pea   *pois*

**Peas** are vegetables.
*Les **pois** sont des légumes.*

**Peas** are good to eat.
*Les **pois** sont bons à manger.*

## peach   *pêche*

A **peach** is a fruit.
*La **pêche** est un fruit.*

It has a fuzzy skin.
*Elle a une peau duvetée.*

## peanut
### cacahuète

**Peanuts** are good to eat.
*Les **cacahuètes** sont bonnes à manger.*

## pear   *poire*

A **pear** is a fruit.
*La **poire** est un fruit.*

**Pears** grow on trees.
*Les **poires** poussent sur des arbres.*

## pen
### plume

We write with a **pen** and ink.
*Nous écrivons avec une **plume** et de l'encre.*

## pencil
### crayon

We use a **pencil** for writing.
*Nous utilisons un **crayon** pour écrire.*

65

# penny  *penny*

A **penny** is an English coin.
*Un **penny** est une pièce de monnaie anglaise.*

# people
## *gens, peuple*

1. These **people** form a group.
   *Ces **gens** forment un groupe.*

2. The redskins are a brave **people.**
   *Les Peaux-Rouges sont un **peuple** courageux.*

# perhaps  *peut-être*

The cloud will **perhaps** bring rain.
*Le nuage apportera **peut-être** de la pluie.*

# person  *personne*

A **person** is a man or woman, boy or girl.
*Une **personne** est un homme ou une femme, un garçon ou une fille.*

# piano  *piano*

We hear music when Mother plays the **piano.**
*Nous entendons de la musique quand maman joue du **piano.***

# pick  *pic*
## to pick  *cueillir*

1. The man works with a **pick.**
   *L'homme travaille avec un **pic.***

2. Beth **picks** flowers.
   *Elisabeth **cueille** des fleurs.*

| I pick | I shall pick | I picked |
|--------|--------------|----------|
| *Je cueille* | *Je cueillerai* | *J'ai cueilli* |

# picnic
## *pique-nique*

Our family went on a **picnic.**
*Notre famille est allée en **pique-nique.***

# picture  *image*

The **pictures** in this book are coloured.
*Les **images** de ce livre sont en couleurs.*

# pie  *tarte*

We often have **pie** for dinner.
*Nous avons souvent de la **tarte** au dîner.*

# piece  *morceau*

I cut a **piece** of the pie.
*Je coupe un **morceau** de la tarte.*

# pig  *porc*

A **pig** is an animal.
*Le **porc** est un animal.*

# pigeon  *pigeon*

A **pigeon** is a bird.
*Le **pigeon** est un oiseau.*

The message was sent by carrier **pigeon.**
*Le message a été envoyé par **pigeon** voyageur.*

# pillow
## *oreiller*

I sleep with my head on a **pillow.**
*Je dors avec la tête sur un **oreiller.***

66

## pin   *épingle*
## to pin   *épingler*

1. We fasten things with **pins**.
   *Nous attachons les choses avec des épingles.*

2. Ruth **pinned** a flower on her dress.
   *Ruth a épinglé une fleur sur sa robe.*

| I pin | I shall pin | I pinned |
|---|---|---|
| *J'épingle* | *J'épinglerai* | *J'ai épinglé* |

## pineapple
## *ananas*

A **pineapple** is a big fruit.
*L'ananas est un gros fruit.*

## pink   *rose*

**Pink** is a colour.
*Le rose est une couleur.*

## pint   *pinte*

A **pint** is a measure for liquids.
*Une pinte est une mesure pour les liquides.*

A small milk bottle holds a half **pint**.
*Une petite bouteille de lait contient une demi pinte.*

## pipe
## *tuyau, pipe*

1. Water comes to our house through **pipes**.
   *L'eau arrive à nos maisons dans des tuyaux.*

2. Father smokes a **pipe**.
   *Papa fume la pipe.*

## place   *place*
## to place   *placer*

1. There is a **place** for Bruce at the table.
   *Il y a une place à table pour Bruce.*

2. Where did you **place** the chair?
   *Où avez-vous placé la chaise ?*

| place | I shall place | I placed |
|---|---|---|
| *e place*  | *Je placerai* | *J'ai placé* |

## plain   *simple, clair*

1. I have a **plain** sheet of paper.
   *J'ai une simple feuille de papier.*

2. Is it **plain** to you?
   *Est-ce clair pour vous ?*

## plan   *plan*

Daddy is making **plans** for our holiday.
*Papa fait des plans pour nos vacances.*

## plant   *plante, usine*
## to plant   *planter*

1. This **plant** grows in a pot.
   *Cette plante pousse dans un pot.*

2. We **plant** flowers in the earth.
   *Nous plantons des fleurs dans la terre.*

3. This is a **plant**.
   *Ceci est une usine.*

   Workmen work in **plants**.
   *Les ouvriers travaillent dans les usines.*

| I plant | I shall plant | I planted |
|---|---|---|
| *Je plante* | *Je planterai* | *J'ai planté* |

## plate   *assiette*

I eat from a blue **plate**.
*Je mange dans une assiette bleue.*

## play   *pièce*
## to play   *jouer*

1. We acted in a **play** at school.
   *Nous avons joué dans une pièce à l'école.*

2. We **play** after school.
   *Nous jouons après l'école.*

   My **play**mate and I **play** with our **playthings**.
   *Mon camarade de jeu et moi jouons avec nos jouets.*

| I play | I shall play | I played |
|---|---|---|
| *Je joue* | *Je jouerai* | *J'ai joué* |

## please    s'il vous plaît
## to please    plaire

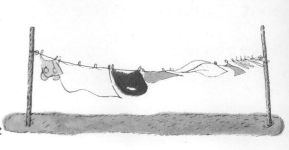

1. Will you **please** give me a biscuit?
   *Voulez-vous, **s'il vous plaît**, me donner un biscuit ?*

2. The toy will **please** the baby.
   *Le jouet **plaira** au bébé.*

| It pleases | It will please | It pleased |
|---|---|---|
| *Cela plaît* | *Cela plaira* | *Cela a plu* |

## plenty of    beaucoup de

We have **plenty of** time to catch the bus.
*Nous avons **beaucoup de** temps pour attraper l'autobus*

## plough    charrue
## to plough    labourer

1. A **plough** is used for turning over the soil.
   *La **charrue** sert à retourner le sol.*

2. The farmer **ploughs** the field.
   *Le fermier **laboure** le champ.*

| I plough | I shall plough | I ploughed |
|---|---|---|
| *Je laboure* | *Je labourerai* | *J'ai labouré* |

## plum    prune

A **plum** is a juicy fruit.
*La **prune** est un fruit juteux.*

**Plums** are good to eat.
*Les **prunes** sont bonnes à manger.*

## pocket    poche

Bill has a handkerchief in his **pocket**.
*Bill a un mouchoir dans sa **poche**.*

## point    pointe
## to point    pointer

1. The **point** of the pencil is the sharp end.
   *La **pointe** du crayon est l'extrémité pointue.*

2. The church spire **points** to the sky.
   *Le clocher de l'église **pointe** vers le ciel.*

| It points | It will point | It pointed |
|---|---|---|
| *Cela pointe* | *Cela pointera* | *Cela a pointé* |

## pole    poteau

The **pole** holds up the clothes-line.
*Le **poteau** soutient la corde à linge.*

## policeman
## agent de police

A **policeman** keeps order among people.
*Un **agent de police** maintient l'ordre parmi les passants.*

He helps us to cross the street.
*Il nous aide à traverser la rue.*

## polite    poli

A **polite** person is pleasant and well-behaved.
*Une personne **polie** est agréable et bien élevée.*

## pony    poney

A **pony** is a small horse.
*Un **poney** est un petit cheval.*

## poor    pauvre

**Poor** people have not much money.
*Les gens **pauvres** n'ont pas beaucoup d'argent.*

## possible    possible

Is it **possible** to fly to the moon?
*Est-il **possible** de voler jusqu'à la lune ?*

Is it **possible** that George is ill?
*Est-il **possible** que Georges soit malade ?*

## post   *poteau, poste*

1. The **post** is stuck in the ground.
   *Le poteau est enfoncé dans le sol.*

2. The **post** office sells us stamps.
   *La poste nous vend des timbres.*

The **postman** delivers our letters.
*Le facteur apporte nos lettres.*

## pot   *pot*

We keep many different things in **pots**.
*Nous conservons beaucoup de choses différentes dans des pots.*

## potato   *pomme de terre*

**Potatoes** are vegetables.
*Les pommes de terre sont des légumes.*

**Potatoes** grow in the ground.
*Les pommes de terre poussent dans la terre.*

## pound   *livre*

1. A **pound** is a measure of weight.
   *La livre est une mesure de poids.*

2. A **pound** is a kind of money.
   *La livre sterling est une monnaie.*

## to pour   *verser*

Lucy **pours** the milk from the jug into the glass.
*Lucie verse le lait de la cruche dans le verre.*

| I pour | I shall pour | I poured |
|---|---|---|
| Je verse | Je verserai | J'ai versé |

## to pray   *prier*

When we **pray** we talk to God.
*Quand nous prions nous parlons à Dieu.*

| I pray | I shall pray | I prayed |
|---|---|---|
| Je prie | Je prierai | J'ai prié |

## prayer   *prière*

Ellen is saying her **prayers**.
*Hélène récite ses prières.*

## present   *présent, cadeau*

1. Today is in the **present**.
   *Aujourd'hui est dans le présent.*

   Yesterday is in the past.
   *Hier est dans le passé.*

2. There are **presents** under the tree.
   *Il y a des cadeaux sous l'arbre.*

## president   *président*

A **president** is leader of a country.
*Un président est le chef d'un pays.*

George Washington was the first **president** of the United States.
*George Washington fut le premier président des États-Unis.*

## to press   *appuyer, repasser*

1. Ruth will **press** the switch to turn on the light.
   *Pour allumer, Ruth appuyera sur l'interrupteur.*

2. Mother **presses** the clothes with an iron.
   *Maman repasse les vêtements avec un fer.*

| I press | I shall press | I pressed |
|---|---|---|
| J'appuie | J'appuierai | J'ai appuyé |
| Je repasse | Je repasserai | J'ai repassé |

## pretty   *joli*

Mary had a **pretty** ribbon in her hair.
*Marie avait un joli ruban dans les cheveux.*

## price   *prix*

What is the **price** of the book?
*Quel est le prix du livre ?*

## prince   *prince*

A **prince** is the son of a king and a queen.
*Un prince est le fils d'un roi et d'une reine.*

## princess   *princesse*

A **princess** is the daughter of a king and a queen.
*Une princesse est la fille d'un roi et d'une reine.*

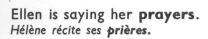

69

## print  *trace*
## to print  *imprimer*

1. Rover left foot**prints**.
   *Rover a laissé des **traces** de pattes.*

2. This book was **printed** on a printing press.
   *Ce livre a été **imprimé** sur une presse d'imprimerie.*

| I print | I shall print | I printed |
|---------|---------------|-----------|
| *J'imprime* | *J'imprimerai* | *J'ai imprimé* |

## pudding  *pudding*

**Pudding** is a dessert.
*Le **pudding** est un entremets.*

## to pull  *tirer*

Tom **pulls** his cart.
*Tom **tire** son chariot.*

| I pull | I shall pull | I pulled |
|--------|--------------|----------|
| *Je tire* | *Je tirerai* | *J'ai tiré* |

## pumpkin  *potiron*

A **pumpkin** grows near the ground.
*Le **potiron** pousse près du sol.*

People make jack-o'-lanterns from **pumpkins** at Hallowe'en.
*Les gens font des lampions dans les **potirons** à l'occasion de Hallowe'en.*

## puppy  *chiot*

A **puppy** is a young dog.
*Un **chiot** est un jeune chien.*

# Q q

Seventeenth letter of the alphabet.
*Dix-septième lettre de l'alphabet.*

## quarry  *carrière*

Marble is dug from **quarries**.
*Le marbre est extrait des **carrières**.*

## purple  *violet*

**Purple** is a colour.
*Le **violet** est une couleur.*

## purse
## *porte-monnaie*

Mother keeps her money in a **purse**.
*Maman garde son argent dans un **porte-monnaie**.*

## to push  *pousser*

Ann pushes the **pram**.
*Anne **pousse** la voiture d'enfant.*

| I push | I shall push | I pushed |
|--------|--------------|----------|
| *Je pousse* | *Je pousserai* | *J'ai poussé* |

## to put  *mettre*

Tom **puts** his hat on his head.
*Tom **met** son chapeau sur sa tête.*

| I put | I shall put | I put |
|-------|-------------|-------|
| *Je mets* | *Je mettrai* | *J'ai mis* |

## puzzle  *puzzle*

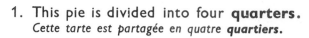

Ann and Bob have a **puzzle**.
*Anne et Bob ont un **puzzle**.*

## quarter  *quartier, quart*

1. This pie is divided into four **quarters**.
   *Cette tarte est partagée en quatre **quartiers**.*

2. We eat dinner at **quarter** past seven.
   *Nous dînons à sept heures et **quart**.*

## queen  *reine*

A **queen** is the wife of a king.
*Une **reine** est la femme d'un roi.*

Sometimes she reigns alone.
*Quelquefois elle règne toute seule.*

## question  *question*

We ask a **question** when we want to know something.
*Nous posons une **question** quand nous voulons savoir quelque chose.*

Is it raining? is a **question**.
*Pleut-il? est une **question**.*

## quick  *vif, vite*

To be **quick** is to do something fast.
*Être **vif**, c'est faire quelque chose vite.*

Tom ran **quickly**.
*Tom courait **vite**.*

## quiet  *silencieux, tranquille*

1. To be **quiet** is to make no noise.
   *Être **silencieux**, c'est ne pas faire de bruit.*

2. Jack is **quiet** because he is asleep.
   *Jacques est **tranquille** parce qu'il dort.*

## quite  *tout à fait*

The glass is **quite** full.
*Le verre est **tout à fait** plein.*

The rose is **quite** red.
*La rose est **tout à fait** rouge.*

---

# R r

Eighteenth letter of the alphabet.
*Dix-huitième lettre de l'alphabet.*

## rabbit  *lapin*

A **rabbit** is an animal with fur.
*Le **lapin** est un animal à fourrure.*

It has long ears.
*Il a de longues oreilles.*

## race  *course*

The boys had a **race** to see who could run the fastest.
*Les garçons ont fait une **course** pour voir qui courait le plus vite.*

## radio  *radio*

We hear voices and music over the **radio**.
*Nous entendons des voix et de la musique à la **radio**.*

## rail  *rail*

The train runs on **rails**.
*Le train roule sur des **rails**.*

## rain  *pluie*

The **rain** comes down in drops of water.
*La **pluie** tombe sous forme de gouttes d'eau.*

## rainbow  *arc-en-ciel*

See the **rainbow** in the sky!
*Voyez l'**arc-en-ciel** dans le ciel!*

## rat  *rat*

A **rat** is a small animal.
*Le **rat** est un petit animal.*

It has a long tail.
*Il a une longue queue.*

## rather  *plutôt*

It is **rather** cold.
*Il fait **plutôt** froid.*

## to reach  *atteindre*

Bruce is trying to **reach** the bin.
*Bruce essaie d'**atteindre** la boîte.*

| I reach | I shall reach | I reached |
|---------|---------------|-----------|
| *J'atteins* | *J'atteindrai* | *J'ai atteint* |

# to read    lire

We **read** stories in books.
*Nous **lisons** des histoires dans les livres.*

| I read | I shall read | I read |
|--------|--------------|--------|
| *Je lis* | *Je lirai* | *J'ai lu* |

# ready    prêt

Are you **ready** for school?
*Êtes-vous **prêt** pour aller à l'école ?*

# really    vraiment

It is **really** cold today.
*Il fait **vraiment** froid aujourd'hui.*

# reason    raison

Why did you close the window?
*Pourquoi avez-vous fermé la fenêtre ?*

What was your **reason** for closing it?
*Quelle **raison** aviez-vous pour la fermer ?*

# red
# rouge

**Red** is a colour.
*Le **rouge** est une couleur.*

When the traffic light is **red,** it means STOP.
*Quand le feu est **rouge** cela signifie : "arrêtez-vous".*

# refrigerator
# réfrigérateur

A **refrigerator** keeps food cold.
*Le **réfrigérateur** garde les aliments froids.*

# reindeer    renne

A **reindeer** is an animal which lives in the cold north.
*Le **renne** est un animal qui vit dans le nord glacé.*

# to remember
# se rappeler, se souvenir de

1. I **remember** my vacation.
   *Je **me rappelle** mes vacances.*

2. Did you **remember** to bring your book?
   *Vous êtes-**vous souvenu** d'apporter votre livre ?*

| I remember | I shall remember | I remembered |
|------------|------------------|--------------|
| *Je me rappelle* | *Je me rappellerai* | *Je me suis rappelé* |
| *Je me souviens* | *Je me souviendrai* | *Je me suis souvenu* |

# reply    réponse
# to reply    répondre

1. Father wrote me a letter.
   *Papa m'a écrit une lettre.*

   I will write a **reply** to it.
   *J'écrirai une **réponse** à la lettre.*

2. "Is it raining?" asked Mother.
   *"Pleut-il ?" demanda maman.*

   "Yes, Mother", **replied** John.
   *"Oui, maman", **répondit** Jean.*

| I reply | I shall reply | I replied |
|---------|---------------|-----------|
| *Je réponds* | *Je répondrai* | *J'ai répondu* |

# rest
# repos, reste

1. The tired dog takes a **rest**.
   *Le chien fatigué prend du **repos**.*

2. One apple is on the table.
   *Il y a une pomme sur la table.*

   The **rest** of the apples are in the basket.
   *Le **reste** des pommes est dans le panier.*

# to return    revenir, rendre

1. Father went away last week.
   *Papa est parti la semaine dernière.*

   He will **return** tomorrow.
   *Il **reviendra** demain.*

2. I shall **return** the book tomorrow.
   *Je **rendrai** le livre demain.*

| I return | I shall return | I returned |
|----------|----------------|------------|
| *Je reviens* | *Je reviendrai* | *Je suis revenu* |
| *Je rends* | *Je rendrai* | *J'ai rendu* |

# ribbon
# ruban

We use pretty **ribbons** for tying things.
*Nous employons de jolis **rubans** pour attacher les objets.*

## rice
## riz

**Rice** is a cereal.
*Le riz est une céréale.*

It grows in wet earth.
*Il pousse dans la terre humide.*

## rich   *riche*

The **rich** man has a lot of money.
*L'homme riche a beaucoup d'argent.*

## right   *droit, juste*

1. I have a **right** hand and a left hand.
   *J'ai une main droite et une main gauche.*

2. The ball fell **right** into the basket.
   *La balle tomba juste dans le panier.*

## ring   *bague*
## to ring   *sonner*

1. Mother's **ring** has a jewel in it.
   *Il y a une pierre précieuse sur la bague de maman.*

2. The bells **ring** on Christmas Day.
   *Les cloches sonnent le jour de Noël.*

| I ring | I shall ring | I rang |
|---|---|---|
| *Je sonne* | *Je sonnerai* | *J'ai sonné* |

## ripe   *mûr*

When fruit is **ripe**, we can eat it.
*Quand les fruits sont mûrs, nous pouvons les manger.*

When it is not **ripe**, it does not taste good.
*Quand ils ne sont pas mûrs, ils n'ont pas bon goût.*

## to rise   *se lever, s'élever*

You **rise** in the morning.
*Vous vous levez le matin.*

The balloon **rises** in the air.
*Le ballon s'élève dans l'air.*

| I rise | I shall rise | I rose |
|---|---|---|
| *Je me lève* | *Je me lèverai* | *Je me suis levé* |
| *Je m'élève* | *Je m'élèverai* | *Je me suis élevé* |

## river
## rivière

The **river** flows down to the sea.
*La rivière coule vers la mer.*

## road
## route

The cars go along the **road**.
*Les voitures circulent sur la route.*

## roar   *rugissement*
## to roar   *rugir*

1. A **roar** is a loud noise.
   *Un rugissement est un bruit fort.*

2. Did you ever hear a lion **roar**?
   *Avez-vous entendu un lion rugir?*

| I roar | I shall roar | I roared |
|---|---|---|
| *Je rugis* | *Je rugirai* | *J'ai rugi* |

## robin   *rouge-gorge*

A **robin** is a bird with a red breast.
*Le rouge-gorge est un oiseau à poitrine rouge.*

## rock   *rocher*
## to rock   *bercer*

1. A **rock** is a big stone.
   *Un rocher est une grosse pierre.*

2. Jean **rocks** the baby to sleep.
   *Jeanne berce le bébé pour l'endormir.*

| I rock | I shall rock | I rocked |
|---|---|---|
| *Je berce* | *Je bercerai* | *J'ai bercé* |

## roll   *rouleau, petit pain*
## to roll   *faire rouler*

1. We **roll** the hoop down the hill.
   *Nous faisons rouler le cerceau en descendant la colline.*

2. The paper is in a **roll**.
   *Le papier est en rouleau.*

3. Jim has **roller** skates.
   *Jim a des patins à roulettes.*

4. I had a **roll** for breakfast.
   *J'ai eu un petit pain pour le petit déjeuner.*

| I roll | I shall roll | I rolled |
|---|---|---|
| *Je fais rouler* | *Je ferai rouler* | *J'ai fait rouler* |

## roof toit

The house has a red **roof**.
*La maison a un **toit** rouge.*

## room
## chambre, place

1. The **room** is full of furniture.
   *La **chambre** est pleine de meubles.*

2. Is there **room** for Harry in the lorry?
   *Y a-t-il de la **place** pour Henri dans le camion?*

## root racine

The **roots** of plants grow in the earth.
*Les **racines** des plantes poussent dans la terre.*

## rope
## corde

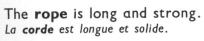

The **rope** is long and strong.
*La **corde** est longue et solide.*

Peter jumps with a **rope**.
*Pierre saute à la **corde**.*

## rose rose

A **rose** is a flower.
*La **rose** est une fleur.*

## rough
## rude, agité, brutal

1. The dog has a **rough** coat.
   *Le chien a une fourrure **rude**.*

2. The ocean is **rough** during a storm.
   *L'océan est **agité** pendant la tempête.*

3. In a **rough** game the boys may get hurt.
   *Dans un jeu **brutal**, les garçons peuvent être blessés.*

## round rond

The ball is **round**.
*La balle est **ronde**.*

## row rangée

The lilies grow in a **row**.
*Les lys poussent sur une **rangée**.*

## to rub effacer

Bill **rubs** the chalk off the board.
*Bill **efface** la craie sur le tableau.*

I rub
*J'efface*

I shall rub
*J'effacerai*

I rubbed
*J'ai effacé*

## rubber
## caoutchouc

We wear **rubber** boots in the rain.
*Nous portons des bottes de **caoutchouc** quand il pleut.*

These things are made from **rubber**.
*Ces objets sont faits en **caoutchouc**.*

## rug tapis

We have a blue **rug** on our floor.
*Nous avons un **tapis** bleu sur notre plancher.*

## rule règle

It is a **rule** in our house to get up early.
*Se lever tôt est la **règle** chez nous.*

## ruler règle

We use a **ruler** to measure length.
*Nous employons une **règle** pour mesurer les longueurs.*

## to run    *courir*

Tom can **run** fast.
*Tom peut **courir** vite.*

| I **run** | I shall **run** | I ran |
|---|---|---|
| *Je cours* | *Je courrai* | *J'ai couru* |

## to rush
## *se dépêcher*

To **rush** means to go in a hurry.
*Se dépêcher signifie se hâter.*

| I **rush** | I shall **rush** | I rushed |
|---|---|---|
| *Je me dépêche* | *Je me dépêcherai* | *Je me suis dépêché* |

# S s

Nineteenth letter of the alphabet.
*Dix-neuvième lettre de l'alphabet.*

## sack    *sac*

The **sack** is full of potatoes.
*Le **sac** est plein de pommes de terre.*

## sad    *triste*

Mary is **sad**
because she has broken her doll.
*Marie est **triste** parce qu'elle a cassé sa poupée.*

## safe    *sûr*

The only **safe** way to cross is to wait for the green light.
*La seule façon **sûre** de traverser est d'attendre le feu vert.*

## sail    *voile*
## to sail    *naviguer*

1. A **sail** is made of cloth.
   *Une **voile** est faite en toile.*

   The wind presses against the **sail**
   and makes the **sailing**-boat move.
   *Le vent pousse la **voile** et fait avancer le bateau à **voiles**.*
2. We like to go **sailing**.
   *Nous aimons **naviguer**.*

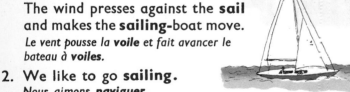

| I **sail** | I shall **sail** | I sailed |
|---|---|---|
| *Je navigue* | *Je naviguerai* | *J'ai navigué* |

## sailor    *marin*

A **sailor** works on a ship.
*Un **marin** travaille sur un navire.*

## salt    *sel*

**Salt** is dug from the earth.
*Le **sel** est extrait de la terre.*

We put **salt** on our food.
*Nous mettons du **sel** dans notre nourriture.*

## same    *même*

My birthday is on May Ist.
*Mon anniversaire est le Ier mai.*

Julie's birthday is on May Ist.
*L'anniversaire de Julie est le Ier mai.*

Our birthdays are on the **same** day.
*Nos anniversaires sont le **même** jour.*

## sand    *sable*

The beach is full of **sand**.
*La plage est pleine de **sable**.*

The children play in the **sand**.
*Les enfants jouent sur le **sable**.*

## sandwich    *sandwich*

I make a **sandwich** with bread and ham.
*Je fais un **sandwich** avec du pain et du jambon.*

## Santa Claus    *Père Noël*

**Santa Claus** comes down the chimney on Christmas Eve.
*Le **Père Noël** descend dans la cheminée la veille de Noël.*

## to save　*sauver*

The man swam to **save** the boy.
*L'homme nageait pour **sauver** le petit garçon.*

| I save | I shall save | I saved |
|---|---|---|
| *Je sauve* | *Je sauverai* | *J'ai sauvé* |

## saw　*scie*

A **saw** is used for cutting wood.
*La **scie** sert à couper le bois.*

## scale　*balance, écaille*

1. A **scale** is used to weigh things.
   *Une **balance** sert à peser les objets.*

   A pound of sugar is on the **scale**.
   *Il y a une livre de sucre sur la **balance**.*

2. Some fish are covered with **scales**.
   *Certains poissons sont couverts d'**écailles**.*

## school　*école*

We go to **school** to learn.
*Nous allons à l'**école** pour nous instruire.*

## scissors　*ciseaux*

Scissors are used for cutting.
*Les **ciseaux** servent à couper.*

## scratch　*éraflure*
## to scratch　*gratter*

1. The cat made a **scratch** on the chair.
   *Le chat a fait une **éraflure** à la chaise.*

2. We can **scratch** with our fingernails.
   *Nous pouvons **gratter** avec nos ongles.*

| I scratch | I shall scratch | I scratched |
|---|---|---|
| *Je gratte* | *Je gratterai* | *J'ai gratté* |

## screw　*vis*
## to screw　*visser*

1. This is a **screw**.
   *Voici une **vis**.*

2. **Screws** are used to hold things together.
   *Les **vis** servent à assembler les objets.*

   **Screw** the top on the jar of jam.
   *Vissez le couvercle sur le pot de confiture.*

| I screw | I shall screw | I screwed |
|---|---|---|
| *Je visse* | *Je visserai* | *J'ai vissé* |

## to scrub　*frotter*

Annie **scrubs** the floor with a brush.
*Annie **frotte** le plancher avec une brosse.*

| I scrub | I shall scrub | I scrubbed |
|---|---|---|
| *Je frotte* | *Je frotterai* | *J'ai frotté* |

## sea　*mer*

The **sea** is full of salt water.
*La **mer** est remplie d'eau salée.*

Ships sail on the **sea**.
*Les bateaux voguent sur la **mer**.*

## season　*saison*

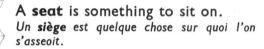

There are four **seasons** in the year.
*Il y a quatre **saisons** dans l'année.*

They are spring, summer, autumn and winter.
*Ce sont le printemps, l'été, l'automne et l'hiver.*

## seat　*siège*

A **seat** is something to sit on.
*Un **siège** est quelque chose sur quoi l'on s'asseoit.*

## to see　*voir*

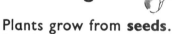

We **see** with our eyes.
*Nous **voyons** avec nos yeux.*

When our eyes are closed we cannot **see**.
*Quand nos yeux sont fermés nous ne pouvons pas **voir**.*

| I see | I shall see | I saw |
|---|---|---|
| *Je vois* | *Je verrai* | *J'ai vu* |

## seed　*graine*

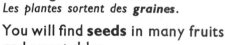

Plants grow from **seeds**.
*Les plantes sortent des **graines**.*

You will find **seeds** in many fruits and vegetables.
*Vous trouverez des **graines** dans beaucoup de fruits et de légumes.*

## to seem　*sembler, paraître*

1. What the dog saw in the mirror **seemed** to be another dog.
   *Ce que le chien voyait dans la glace **semblait** être un autre chien.*

2. The weather **seems** better today.
   *Le temps **paraît** meilleur aujourd'hui.*

| I seem | I shall seem | I seemed |
|---|---|---|
| *Je semble* | *Je semblerai* | *J'ai semblé* |
| *Je parais* | *Je paraîtrai* | *J'ai paru* |

## to sell    *vendre*

The grocer **sells** groceries.
*L'épicier **vend** des produits d'épicerie.*

| I sell | I shall sell | I sold |
|---|---|---|
| *Je vends* | *Je vendrai* | *J'ai vendu* |

## to send    *envoyer*

I will **send** a letter.
*J'**enverrai** une lettre.*

Mother **sent** me to the shop.
*Maman m'**a envoyé** à la boutique.*

| I send | I shall send | I sent |
|---|---|---|
| *J'envoie* | *J'enverrai* | *J'ai envoyé* |

## to set    *poser, se coucher*

1. The things are **set** on the table.
   *Les choses sont **posées** sur la table.*

2. The sun is **setting**.
   *Le soleil se **couche**.*

| I set | I shall set | I set |
|---|---|---|
| *Je pose* | *Je poserai* | *J'ai posé* |

| It sets | It will set | It set |
|---|---|---|
| *Il se couche* | *Il se couchera* | *Il s'est couché* |

## seven    *sept*

**7**

**Seven** is a number.
***Sept** est un nombre.*

Here are **seven** ducks.
*Voici **sept** canards.*

## to sew    *coudre*

We **sew** cloth.
*Nous **cousons** l'étoffe.*

Mother **is sewing** her dress.
*Maman **coud** sa robe.*

| I sew | I shall sew | I sewed |
|---|---|---|
| *Je couds* | *Je coudrai* | *J'ai cousu* |

## shade    *ombre*

It is cooler in the **shade** than in the sun.
*Il fait plus frais à l'**ombre** qu'au soleil.*

## shadow *ombre*

Betty's **shadow** is on the wall.
*L'**ombre** de Betty est sur le mur.*

## to shake    *secouer*

Mother **shakes** the dust out
of the rug.
*Maman **secoue** la poussière du tapis.*

| I shake | I shall shake | I shook |
|---|---|---|
| *Je secoue* | *Je secouerai* | *J'ai secoué* |

## to shake hands
## *serrer la main*

We **shake hands** when we meet our
friends.
*Quand nous rencontrons nos amis nous leur
**serrons** la main.*

| I shake hands | I shall shake hands | I shook hands |
|---|---|---|
| *Je serre la main* | *Je serrerai la main* | *J'ai serré la main* |

## shape
## *forme*

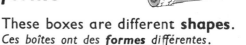

These boxes are different **shapes**.
*Ces boîtes ont des **formes** différentes.*

## share    *part*
## to share    *partager*

1. We **share** the biscuits.
   *Nous **partageons** les biscuits.*

2. I gave my **share** to Bruce.
   *J'ai donné ma **part** à Bruce.*

| I share | I shall share | I shared |
|---|---|---|
| *Je partage* | *Je partagerai* | *J'ai partagé* |

## sharp    *aigu, aiguisé, coupant*
## to sharpen    *aiguiser*

1. The pencil point is **sharp**.
   *La pointe du crayon est **aiguisée**.*

2. The knife is **sharp**.
   *Le canif est **coupant**.*

3. We cut with the **sharp** edge of the knife.
   *Nous coupons avec la lame **aiguë** du canif.*

| I sharpen | I shall sharpen | I sharpened |
|---|---|---|
| *J'aiguise* | *J'aiguiserai* | *J'ai aiguisé* |

## she   elle

This is Ann.
*Voici Anne.*

**She** has a doll.
*Elle a une poupée.*

**She** plays by herself with her doll.
*Elle joue toute seule avec sa poupée.*

| she | her | hers |
|---|---|---|
| *elle* | *elle, la, lui, son, sa, ses* | *le sien, la sienne* |

## sheep
## mouton

A **sheep** is an animal.
*Le mouton est un animal.*

**Sheep** provide us with wool.
*Les moutons nous fournissent de la laine.*

## shelf   étagère

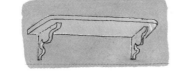

The **shelf** is painted green.
*L'étagère est peinte en vert.*

## shell
## coquille,  coquillages

1. Some sea animals are covered with **shells**.
   *Certains animaux marins sont recouverts d'une coquille.*

   An egg has a **shell**.
   *L'œuf a une coquille.*

2. We find **seashells** on the beach.
   *Nous trouvons des coquillages sur la plage.*

## to shine
## briller, faire briller

1. The moon **shines** on the water.
   *La lune brille sur l'eau.*

2. Peter **shines** his shoes.
   *Pierre fait briller ses souliers.*

| I shine | I shall shine | I shone |
|---|---|---|
| *Je brille* | *Je brillerai* | *J'ai brillé* |
| *Je fais briller* | *Je ferai briller* | *J'ai fait briller* |

## ship   bateau

**Ships** sail on the sea.
*Les bateaux voguent sur la mer.*

## shirt   chemise

Men and boys wear **shirts**.
*Les hommes et les garçons portent des chemises.*

## shoe
## chaussure

We wear **shoes** on our feet.
*Nous portons des chaussures à nos pieds.*

## to shoot
## tirer

Bill **shoots** his gun.
*Bill tire avec son fusil.*

| I shoot | I shall shoot | I shot |
|---|---|---|
| *Je tire* | *Je tirerai* | *J'ai tiré* |

## shop   magasin
## to shop   faire des courses

1. Ann and Peter went **shopping**.
   *Anne et Pierre sont allés faire des courses.*

2. They are in the **shop**.
   *Ils sont dans le magasin.*

| I shop | I shall shop | I shopped |
|---|---|---|
| *Je fais des courses* | *Je ferai des courses* | *J'ai fait des courses* |

## shore
## rivage

The **shore** is by the edge of the sea.
*Le rivage est au bord de la mer.*

## short
## court

The red ribbon is **short**.
*Le ruban rouge est court.*

## shoulder   épaule

The bird perched on the man's **shoulder**.
*L'oiseau s'est perché sur l'épaule de l'homme.*

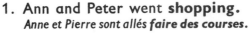

## shovel
## pelle

Ed cleaned the path
with a snow **shovel**.
*Ed a nettoyé le sentier avec une **pelle** à neige.*

A steam **shovel** digs big holes.
*Une **pelle** mécanique creuse de grands trous.*

## to show     montrer

I will **show** you my rabbit.
*Je vous **montrerai** mon lapin.*

| I show | I shall show | I showed |
|--------|--------------|----------|
| *Je montre* | *Je montrerai* | *J'ai montré* |

## sick     malade

Tom feels **sick**.
*Tom se sent **malade**.*

## side     côté

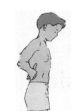

My right arm is on my right **side**.
*Mon bras droit est à mon **côté** droit.*

My left arm is on my left **side**.
*Mon bras gauche est à mon **côté** gauche.*

## sign     signe
## to sign     signer

1. A **sign** tells us something.
   *Un **signe** nous indique quelque chose.*

   This **sign** tells the way to town.
   *Ce **signe** montre le chemin de la ville.*

2. Can you **sign** your name?
   *Pouvez-vous **signer** votre nom?*

| I sign | I shall sign | I signed |
|--------|--------------|----------|
| *Je signe* | *Je signerai* | *J'ai signé* |

## silent     silencieux

The house was **silent**.
*La maison était **silencieuse**.*

## silk
## soie

**Silk** thread is made by **silkworms**.
*Le fil de **soie** est fait par les **vers à soie**.*

We make **silk** into cloth.
*Nous faisons de l'étoffe avec de la **soie**.*

## silver
## argent

**Silver** is a metal.
*L'**argent** est un métal.*

Mother has spoons, forks and
other things made of **silver**.

*Maman a des cuillères, des fourchettes
et d'autres objets en **argent**.*

## to sing     chanter

Can you **sing** a song?
*Pouvez-vous **chanter** une chanson?*

| I sing | I shall sing | I sang |
|--------|-------------|--------|
| *Je chante* | *Je chanterai* | *J'ai chanté* |

## sink     évier
## to sink     couler

1. The water runs down the **sink**.
   *L'eau coule dans l'**évier**.*

2. The ship **sinks**.
   *Le bateau **coule**.*

| I sink | I shall sink | I sank |
|--------|-------------|--------|
| *Je coule* | *Je coulerai* | *J'ai coulé* |

## sister     sœur

Betty is my **sister**.
*Betty est ma **sœur**.*

## to sit     s'asseoir

I **sit** on a chair.
*Je m'**asseois** sur une chaise.*

| I sit | I shall sit | I sat |
|-------|------------|-------|
| *Je m'asseois* | *Je m'assiérai* | *Je me suis assis* |

## six     six     6

**Six** is a number.
*Six est un nombre.*

Here are **six** bunnies.
*Voici **six** lapereaux.*

## size    taille

What **size** is your coat?
*Quelle est la **taille** de votre manteau?*

The brown dog is of a larger **size**
than the white dog.
*Le chien brun est d'une plus grande **taille** que le chien blanc.*

## skate    patin
## to skate    patiner

1. We wear **skates** on our feet.
   *Nous mettons des **patins** aux pieds.*

2. We will **skate** on the ice.
   *Nous **patinerons** sur la glace.*

| I skate | I shall skate | I skated |
|---|---|---|
| *Je patine* | *Je patinerai* | *J'ai patiné* |

## skin    peau

Our bodies are covered with **skin**.
*Nos corps sont recouverts de **peau**.*

An orange has a thick **skin**.
*L'orange a une **peau** épaisse.*

## to skip
## sauter à la corde

Lily **skips** with a rope.
*Lily **saute à la corde**.*

| I skip | I shall skip | I skipped |
|---|---|---|
| *Je saute* | *Je sauterai* | *J'ai sauté* |
| *à la corde* | *à la corde* | *à la corde* |

## sky    ciel

We see the sun, moon, stars
and clouds in the **sky**.

*Nous voyons le soleil, la lune,
les étoiles et les nuages dans le **ciel**.*

## sleep    sommeil
## to sleep
## dormir, s'endormir

Ann **went to sleep** and **slept** well, in a deep **sleep**.
*Anne **s'est endormie** et **dormait** bien, d'un profond **sommeil**.*

| I sleep | I shall sleep | I slept |
|---|---|---|
| *Je dors* | *Je dormirai* | *J'ai dormi* |
| *Je m'endors* | *Je m'endormirai* | *Je me suis endormi* |

## sleigh    traîneau

We ride over the snow
in a **sleigh**.

*Nous avançons sur la neige
dans un **traîneau**.*

## slide    pente
## to slide    glisser

1. Tom and Ann **slide** on the ice.
   *Tom et Anne **glissent** sur la glace.*

2. I **slide** down the **slide**.
   *Je **glisse** en descendant la **pente**.*

| I slide | I shall slide | I slid |
|---|---|---|
| *Je glisse* | *Je glisserai* | *J'ai glissé* |

## slip    petite bande (de papier)
## to slip    glisser

1. Write your name on a **slip of paper**.
   *Écrivez votre nom sur une **petite bande de papier**.*

2. Bill's foot **slipped**.
   *Le pied de Bill a **glissé**.*

| I slip | I shall slip | I slipped |
|---|---|---|
| *Je glisse* | *Je glisserai* | *J'ai glissé* |

## slow    lent

The tortoise is **slow**.
*La tortue est **lente**.*

The tortoise goes **slowly**.
*La tortue marche **lentement**.*

## small
## petit

A pea is **small**.
*Un pois est **petit**.*

## smell    odeur
## to smell    sentir

1. The rose has a sweet **smell**.
   *La rose a une **odeur** agréable.*

2. We **smell** with our noses.
   *Nous **sentons** avec notre nez.*

| I smell | I shall smell | I smelled |
|---|---|---|
| *Je sens* | *Je sentirai* | *J'ai senti* |

## to smile    sourire

We **smile** when we are happy.
*Nous **sourions** quand nous sommes heureux.*

Bob is **smiling**.
*Bob **sourit**.*

| I smile | I shall smile | I smiled |
|---|---|---|
| *Je souris* | *Je sourirai* | *J'ai souri* |

# smoke    *fumée*
# to smoke    *fumer*

1. Grey **smoke** goes up from the fire.
   *Une **fumée** grise monte du feu.*

2. Father **smokes** a pipe.
   *Papa **fume** la pipe.*

| I smoke | I shall smoke | I smoked |
|---|---|---|
| *Je fume* | *Je fumerai* | *J'ai fumé* |

# smooth    *doux*

Silk is **smooth** to touch.
*La soie est **douce** au toucher.*

# snail    *escargot*

The **snail** has a shell on his back.
*L'**escargot** a une coquille sur le dos.*

# snake    *serpent*

The **snake** is an animal with no legs.
*Le **serpent** est un animal sans jambes.*

The **snake** crawls along.
*Le **serpent** rampe.*

# to sneeze    *éternuer*

Tom's cold made him **sneeze**, "Atchoo".
*Le rhume de Tom l'a fait **éternuer** : "Atchoum!"*

| I sneeze | I shall sneeze | I sneezed |
|---|---|---|
| *J'éternue* | *J'éternuerai* | *J'ai éternué* |

# snow    *neige*

**Snow** appears in winter.
*La **neige** apparaît en hiver.*

It falls in white flakes.
*Elle tombe en flocons blancs.*

# so    *si, aussi, ainsi*

1. Rover ran **so** fast that he got tired.
   *Rover courait **si** vite qu'il s'est fatigué.*

2. I will go and **so** will you.
   *J'irai et vous **aussi**.*

3. Do you think it is **so**?
   *Croyez-vous que ce soit **ainsi**?*

# soap    *savon*

We wash things with **soap**.
*Nous lavons les objets avec du **savon**.*

# sock    *chaussette*

We wear **socks** on our feet.
*Nous portons des **chaussettes** aux pieds.*

# soft    *mou, molle*

The cushion is **soft**.
*Le coussin est **mou**.*

The snow was **soft**.
*La neige était **molle**.*

# soldier    *soldat*

The **soldier** is in the army.
*Le **soldat** est dans l'armée.*

# some    *quelque*

Some of the apples are green.
*Quelques-unes des pommes sont vertes.*

Some people came at four o'clock.
*Quelques personnes sont venues à quatre heures.*

# something    *quelque chose*

**Something** is in the box.
*Il y a **quelque chose** dans la boîte.*

What is it?
*Qu'est-ce que c'est?*

# sometimes    *quelquefois*

**Sometimes** there is a rainbow.
*Quelquefois il y a un arc-en-ciel.*

# son    *fils*

Bill is the **son** of his father and his mother.
*Bill est le **fils** de son père et de sa mère.*

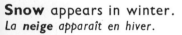
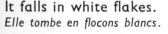

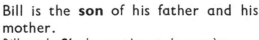

## song  *chanson*

We sing a **song**.
*Nous chantons une chanson.*

## soon  *bientôt*

**Soon** it will be dinner time.
*Bientôt ce sera l'heure du dîner.*

## to sort  *trier*

Harry **sorts** his marbles.
*Henri trie ses billes.*

He puts the green ones together and the brown ones together.
*Il met les vertes ensemble et les brunes ensemble.*

| I sort | I shall sort | I sorted |
|---|---|---|
| *Je trie* | *Je trierai* | *J'ai trié* |

## sound  *son*

I hear the **sound** of voices.
*J'entends le son des voix.*

## soup  *soupe*

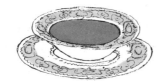

**Soup** is a liquid food.
*La soupe est un mets liquide.*

I had a bowl of tomato **soup**.
*J'ai eu un bol de soupe à la tomate.*

## south  *sud*

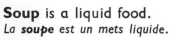

**South** is a direction.
*Le sud est une direction.*

**South** is opposite to north.
*Le sud est l'opposé du nord.*

The birds fly **south** in the winter.
*Les oiseaux volent vers le sud en hiver.*

## spade  *bêche*

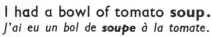

We dig with a **spade**.
*Nous creusons avec une bêche.*

## to speak  *parler*

Peter **speaks** to the class.
*Pierre parle aux élèves.*

He tells them about his trip.
*Il leur parle de son voyage.*

| I speak | I shall speak | I spoke |
|---|---|---|
| *Je parle* | *Je parlerai* | *J'ai parlé* |

## to spill  *renverser*

Bill **spills** a glass of water
*Bill renverse un verre d'eau.*

| I spill | I shall spill | I spilled |
|---|---|---|
| *Je renverse* | *Je renverserai* | *J'ai renversé* |

## spoon  *cuillère*

We eat with a **spoon**.
*Nous mangeons avec une cuillère.*

## spot  *tache*
## to spot  *tacher*

1. The ink made a **spot** on the cloth.
   *L'encre a fait une tache sur la nappe.*

2. The leopard has a **spotted** coat.
   *Le léopard a une fourrure tachetée.*

| I spot | I shall spot | I spotted |
|---|---|---|
| *Je tache* | *Je tacherai* | *J'ai taché* |

## spring
## *printemps*  *ressort*

1. The flowers bloom
   in the **spring**.
   *Les fleurs fleurissent au printemps.*

2. The **spring** came out of the watch.
   *Le ressort est sorti de la montre.*

## square  *carré*

A chess board is **square**.
*Un échiquier est carré.*

## stairs  *escalier*

The **stairs** are painted red.
*L'escalier est peint en rouge.*

# stamp    timbre

The letter has a **stamp** in the corner.
*Il y a un **timbre** dans le coin de la lettre.*

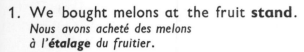

# stand    étalage
# to stand    se tenir debout

1. We bought melons at the fruit **stand**.
   *Nous avons acheté des melons
   à l'**étalage** du fruitier.*

2. I **stand** on two legs.
   *Je **me tiens debout** sur mes deux jambes.*

| I stand | I shall stand | I stood |
|---|---|---|
| *Je me tiens debout* | *Je me tiendrai debout* | *Je me suis tenu debout* |

# star    étoile

The **stars** shine at night.
*Les **étoiles** brillent la nuit.*

# state    état

Here is the map of the United **States**.

*Voici la carte des **États**-Unis.*

# station    gare

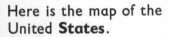

Trains stop at a railway **station**.
*Les trains s'arrêtent à la **gare**.*

# step    pas, marche

1. The baby took his first **steps**.
   *Le bébé a fait ses premiers **pas**.*

2. The staircase has fifteen **steps**.
   *L'escalier a quinze **marches**.*

# stick    bâton
# to stick    coller

1. A **stick** is a small piece of wood.
   *Un **bâton** est un petit morceau de bois.*

2. One **sticks** paper with glue.
   *On **colle** du papier avec de la colle.*

| I stick | I shall stick | I stuck |
|---|---|---|
| *Je colle* | *Je collerai* | *J'ai collé* |

# still    calme
# tranquille, encore

1. The water is **still**.
   *L'eau est **calme**.*

2. Rover is **still**.
   *Rover est **tranquille**.*

3. Are you **still** in bed?
   *Etes-vous **encore** au lit?*

# stocking
# bas

We wear **stockings** on our legs.
*Nous portons des **bas** aux jambes.*

# stone    pierre

**Stone** is hard.
*La **pierre** est dure.*

The farmer made a **stone** wall.
*Le fermier fit un mur en **pierres**.*

# to stop    s'arrêter

The car **stops** at the red light.
*La voiture **s'arrête** au feu rouge.*

| I stop | I shall stop | I stopped |
|---|---|---|
| *Je m'arrête* | *Je m'arrêterai* | *Je me suis arrêté* |

# store    magasin
# to store    entasser

1. We find many things in **stores**.
   *On trouve beaucoup d'objets dans
   les **magasins**.*

2. The squirrel **stores** nuts.
   *L'écureuil **entasse** les noisettes.*

| I store | I shall store | I stored |
|---|---|---|
| *J'entasse* | *J'entasserai* | *J'ai entassé* |

# storm    tempête

During a **storm** it rains
and blows and sometimes
snows.
*Pendant la **tempête** il pleut, il fait du vent et quelquefois il neige.*

## story  *histoire*

I like the **story** of Cinderella.
*J'aime l'**histoire** de Cendrillon.*

## stove  *fourneau*

We use **stoves** for cooking.
*Nous utilisons des **fourneaux** pour faire la cuisine.*

## straight
## *droit*

The ruler is **straight**.
*La règle est **droite**.*

## stream
## *ruisseau*

A little river is a **stream**.
*Une petite rivière est un **ruisseau**.*

## street
## *rue*

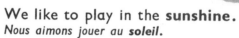

There are houses
on both sides of the **street**.
*Il y a des maisons des deux côtés de la **rue**.*

## string
## *ficelle*

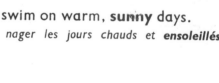

We use **string** for tying things.
*Nous utilisons la **ficelle** pour attacher les objets.*

## strong  *fort, résistant*

1. The **strong** man lifts the weights.
   *L'homme **fort** soulève les poids.*

2. Iron is **strong**.
   *Le fer est **résistant**.*

## such  *tel*

Yesterday we had **such** a storm.
*Hier nous avons eu une **telle** tempête.*

## suddenly
## *tout à coup*

**Suddenly** the sun came out.
***Tout à coup** le soleil apparut.*

## sugar  *sucre*

**Sugar** is sweet.
*Le **sucre** est doux.*

## suit  *costume*

A **suit** is clothing.
*Un **costume** est un vêtement.*

## summer  *été*

**Summer** is the warmest
season of the year.
*L'**été** est la saison la plus chaude
de l'année.*

## sun  *soleil*

The **sun** is setting.
*Le **soleil** se couche.*

We like to play in the **sunshine**.
*Nous aimons jouer au **soleil**.*

We like to swim on warm, **sunny** days.
*Nous aimons nager les jours chauds et **ensoleillés**.*

## supper
## *souper*

**Supper** is the last meal of the day.
*Le **souper** est le dernier repas du jour.*

## to suppose
## *supposer*

Do you **suppose** Father Christmas will come?
***Supposez**-vous que le Père Noël viendra?*

I suppose     I shall suppose     I supposed
*Je suppose*     *Je supposerai*     *J'ai supposé*

## sure    *certain*

"Has the rain stopped?"
*" La pluie s'est-elle arrêtée?"*
"I will look to make **sure**".
*" Je vais regarder pour en être **certain** ".*

## surprise    *surprise*
## to surprise    *surprendre*

1. Mother had a **surprise** for Jim.
   *Maman avait une **surprise** pour Jim.*
2. He **surprised** her by coming home early.
   *Il la **surprit** en rentrant de bonne heure à la maison.*

| I surprise | I shall surprise | I surprised |
|---|---|---|
| *Je surprends* | *Je surprendrai* | *J'ai surpris* |

## to sweep
## *balayer*

Bill **sweeps** up the dust.
*Bill **balaie** la poussière.*

| I sweep | I shall sweep | I swept |
|---|---|---|
| *Je balaie* | *Je balaierai* | *J'ai balayé* |

# T t

Twentieth letter of the alphabet.
*Vingtième lettre de l'alphabet.*

## table    *table*

A **table** is a piece of furniture.
*La **table** est un meuble.*

## tail    *queue*

Some animals have **tails**.
*Certains animaux ont une **queue**.*
A squirrel has a long bushy **tail**.
*L'écureuil a une longue **queue** touffue.*

## to take
## *emporter    prendre*

1. Sue **takes** her books to school.
   *Suzanne **emporte** ses livres à l'école.*
2. She **takes** them with her.
   *Elle les **prend** avec elle.*

| I take | I shall take | I took |
|---|---|---|
| *J'emporte* | *J'emporterai* | *J'ai emporté* |
| *Je prends* | *Je prendrai* | *J'ai pris* |

## sweet
## *doux, sucré*

1. Sugar is **sweet** to taste.
   *Le sucre est **doux** au gout.*
2. Lemons are not **sweet**.
   *Les citrons ne sont pas **sucrés**.*

These are **sweet** things.
*Voici des choses **sucrées**.*

## to swim    *nager*

Tom **swims** in the water.
*Tom **nage** dans l'eau.*

| I swim | I shall swim | I swam |
|---|---|---|
| *Je nage* | *Je nagerai* | *J'ai nagé* |

## swing    *balançoire*
## to swing    *se balancer*

Lucy **swings** in her **swing**.
*Lucie **se balance** sur sa **balançoire**.*

| I swing | I shall swing | I swung |
|---|---|---|
| *Je me balance* | *Je me balancerai* | *Je me suis balancé* |

## to talk    *parler*

Our baby is learning **to talk**.
*Notre bébé apprend a **parler**.*

| I talk | I shall talk | I talked |
|---|---|---|
| *Je parle* | *Je parlerai* | *J'ai parlé* |

## tall    *grand, haut*

1. Daddy is **tall**.
   *Papa est **grand**.*
2. The building is **tall**.
   *L'édifice est **haut**.*

## taste    *goût*
## to taste    *goûter*

1. Sweets have a good **taste**.
   *Les bonbons ont bon **goût**.*
2. We **taste** with our tongues.
   *Nous **goûtons** avec nos langues.*

| I taste | I shall taste | I tasted |
|---|---|---|
| *Je goûte* | *Je goûterai* | *J'ai goûté* |

## to teach
### enseigner

Mother **teaches** Ann to cook.
*Maman **enseigne** a Anne à faire la cuisine.*

Our teacher **teaches** us our lessons.
*Notre professeur nous **enseigne** nos leçons.*

| I teach | I shall teach | I taught |
|---|---|---|
| *J'enseigne* | *J'enseignerai* | *J'ai enseigné* |

## telephone   *téléphone*
## to telephone   *téléphoner*

We talk to people over the **telephone**.
*Nous parlons aux gens par **téléphone**.*

| I telephone | I shall telephone | I telephoned |
|---|---|---|
| *Je téléphone* | *Je téléphonerai* | *J'ai téléphoné* |

## to tell
### raconter

**Tell** a story to the class.
***Racontez** une histoire à la classe.*

| I tell | I shall tell | I told |
|---|---|---|
| *Je raconte* | *Je raconterai* | *J'ai raconté* |

## ten   **10**
### dix

**Ten** is a number.
***Dix** est un nombre.*

Here are **ten** geese.
*Voici **dix** oies.*

## tent   *tente*

The boys have put up a **tent**.
*Les enfants ont dressé une **tente**.*

## than   *que, de*

1. I am taller **than** you.
   *Je suis plus grand **que** vous.*

2. There are fewer **than** three children in the picture.
   *Il y a moins **de** trois enfants sur l'image.*

## to thank   *remercier*
## thank you   *merci*

"**Thank you** for the sweet," says John.
*"**Merci** pour le bonbon", dit Jean.*

We **thank** people when they are kind.
*Nous **remercions** les gens quand ils sont aimables.*

| I thank | I shall thank | I thanked |
|---|---|---|
| *Je remercie* | *Je remercierai* | *J'ai remercié* |

## that   *ce, cet, cette, ces*

**That** dog is naughty.
***Ce** chien est méchant.*

**That** bird in the sky is a crow.
***Cet** oiseau dans le ciel est un corbeau.*

**That** house is beautiful.
***Cette** maison est belle.*

**Those** birds on the ground are chickens.
***Ces** oiseaux sur le sol sont des poulets.*

## the   *le, la, les*

The **petal** fell off **the** rose.
***Le** pétale est tombé de **la** rose.*

The **cats** chased **the** mouse.
***Les** chats ont poursuivi **la** souris.*

## their   *leur*

Schoolboys carry **their** books in **their** satchels.
*Les écoliers transportent **leurs** livres dans **leur** cartable.*

## theirs   *le leur, la leur, les leurs*

Those books are **theirs**.
*Ces livres sont **les leurs**.*

## them   *les, eux, elles*

I saw **them** on the road.
*Je **les** ai vus sur la route.*

The cookies are for **them**.
*Les biscuits sont pour **eux** (ou pour **elles**).*

## then   *puis, alors*

1. I will read the book.
   *Je lirai le livre.*

   **Then** I will take it back.
   ***Puis** je le rapporterai.*

2. Mother was a little girl **then**.
   *Maman était **alors** une petite fille.*

## there   *là*

We will go **there** by train.
*Nous irons **là** par le train.*

## there is, there are   *il y a*

**There is** a rabbit in the garden.
***Il y a** un lapin dans le jardin.*

**There are** stars in the sky.
***Il y a** des étoiles dans le ciel.*

## they   *ils, elles*

My friends are here.
*Mes amis sont ici.*

**They** have come to play.
***Ils** sont venus jouer.*

| them | their | theirs |
|---|---|---|
| *eux, elles, les* | *leur, leurs* | *le leur, la leur, les leurs* |

## thin    *maigre, mince*

1. The tall man is **thin**.
   *L'homme grand est maigre.*

2. The house had **thin** walls.
   *La maison avait des murs minces.*

## thing    *chose*

A house is a **thing** you can see.
*Une maison est une chose que vous pouvez voir.*

## to think    *penser*

We **think** with our minds.
*Nous pensons avec notre esprit.*

Bob **is thinking** about his homework.
*Bob pense à ses devoirs.*

| I think | I shall think | I thought |
| --- | --- | --- |
| *Je pense* | *Je penserai* | *J'ai pensé* |

## this    *ceci, ce, cet, cette*
## these    *ceux-ci, ces*

1. **This** is a squirrel in the tree.
   *Ceci est un écureuil, dans l'arbre.*

   **These** are bears on the ground.
   *Ceux-ci sont des ours, sur le sol.*

2. **This** bear is talking to its baby.
   *Cet ours parle à son bébé.*

   **This** hat is Father's, **this** scarf is Mother's, and **these** shoes are mine.
   *Ce chapeau est à papa, cette écharpe est à maman, et ces souliers sont à moi.*

## thread    *fil*

Mother uses **thread** for sewing.
*Maman emploie du fil pour coudre.*

## three    *trois*

**Three** is a number.
*Trois est un nombre.*

Here are **three** dogs.
*Voici trois chiens.*

## through    *à travers, par*

1. **Through** the window we see the landscape.
   *A travers la fenêtre, nous voyons le paysage.*

2. Tom goes **through** the doorway.
   *Tom passe par la porte.*

## to throw    *lancer*

Peter **throws** the ball.
*Pierre lance le ballon.*

| I throw | I shall throw | I threw |
| --- | --- | --- |
| *Je lance* | *Je lancerai* | *J'ai lancé* |

## thumb    *pouce*

The **thumb** is shorter than the other fingers.
*Le pouce est plus court que les autres doigts.*

## ticket    *billet*

Pat received a **ticket** when he paid to see the circus.
*Pat a reçu un billet quand il a payé son entrée au cirque.*

## tie    *cravate*
## to tie    *attacher*

1. We gave Father a new **tie**.
   *Nous avons offert à papa une cravate neuve.*

2. Bruce can **tie** his shoelaces.
   *Bruce sait attacher ses lacets de souliers.*

| I tie | I shall tie | I tied |
| --- | --- | --- |
| *J'attache* | *J'attacherai* | *J'ai attaché* |

## time    *heure, temps*

1. The clock tells us what **time** it is.
   *La pendule nous dit quelle heure il est.*

   What **time** does the train leave?
   *A quelle heure le train part-il?*

2. Mother has not **time** to help me.
   *Maman n'a pas le temps de m'aider.*

## to    *à, au*

1. Bill walks from the gate **to** the door.
   *Bill marche du portail à la porte.*

2. Bob went **to** market.
   *Bob est allé au marché.*

## today   *aujourd'hui*

**Today** is my birthday.
*Aujourd'hui c'est mon anniversaire.*

## toe   *orteil*

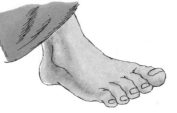

A **toe** is part of the foot.
*Un orteil est une partie du pied.*

I have five **toes** on each foot.
*J'ai cinq orteils à chaque pied.*

## together   *ensemble*

Betty and Ann play **together**.
*Betty et Anne jouent ensemble.*

## tomato   *tomate*

A **tomato** is good to eat.
*La tomate est bonne à manger.*

We grow **tomatoes** in our garden.
*Nous faisons pousser des tomates dans notre jardin.*

## tomorrow   *demain*

**Tomorrow** is the day that comes after today.
*Demain est le jour qui vient après aujourd'hui.*

## tongue   *langue*

Peter put his **tongue** out.
*Pierre a tiré la langue.*

Our **tongues** help us to speak.
*Notre langue nous aide à parler.*

## too   *aussi, trop*

1. May Rover come **too**?
   *Rover peut-il venir aussi?*

2. Mary's soup is **too** hot.
   *La soupe de Marie est trop chaude.*

## tool   *outil*

We use **tools** to work with.
*Nous employons des outils pour travailler.*
These are **tools**.
*Voici des outils.*

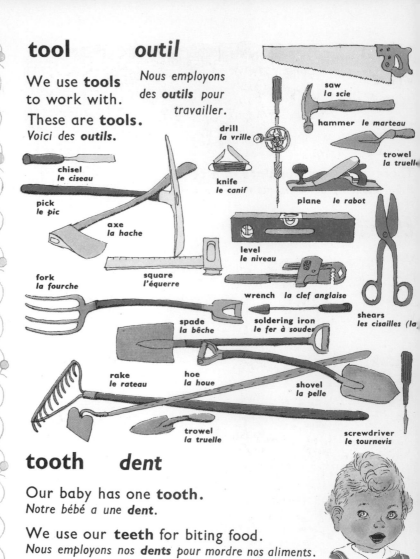

chisel *le ciseau*

pick *le pic*

axe *la hache*

fork *la fourche*

square *l'équerre*

saw *la scie*

hammer *le marteau*

trowel *la truelle*

drill *la vrille*

knife *le canif*

plane *le rabot*

level *le niveau*

wrench *la clef anglaise*

spade *la bêche*

soldering iron *le fer à souder*

shears *les cisailles (la*

rake *le rateau*

hoe *la houe*

shovel *la pelle*

trowel *la truelle*

screwdriver *le tournevis*

## tooth   *dent*

Our baby has one **tooth**.
*Notre bébé a une dent.*

We use our **teeth** for biting food.
*Nous employons nos dents pour mordre nos aliments.*

## top   *haut, en haut de toupie*

1. Robert is sitting on the **top** of the stepladder.
   *Robert est assis au haut de l'échelle.*

   The box is **on top of** the cupboard.
   *La boîte est en haut de l'armoire.*

2. Dick has a red and yellow **top**.
   *Dick a une toupie rouge et jaune.*

## to touch   *toucher*

**Touch** the ice and see how cold it is.
*Touchez la glace et voyez comme elle est froide.*

I touch   I shall touch   I touched
*Je touche*   *Je toucherai*   *J'ai touché*

## towel   *serviette*

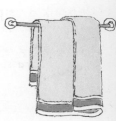

We use a **towel** to dry ourselves.
*Nous employons une serviette pour nous sécher.*

## town
## ville

There are many buildings in a **town**.
*Il y a beaucoup de bâtiments dans une **ville**.*

## toy    jouet

We play with our **toys**.
*Nous jouons avec nos **jouets**.*

These are our **toys**.
*Voici nos **jouets**.*

## tree
## arbre

fir tree
*sapin*

oak tree
*chêne*

apple tree
*pommier*

pa m tree
*paιmier*

These are **trees**.
*Ce sont des **arbres**.*

There are many kinds of **trees**.
*Il y a beaucoup d'espèces d'**arbres**.*

## trip    voyage
## to trip    trébucher

1. We took a **trip** in the country.
   *Nous avons fait un **voyage** à la campagne.*
2. Jim will **trip** on that rug.
   *Jim **trébuchera** sur ce tapis.*

I trip
*e trébuche*

I shall trip
*Je trébucherai*

I tripped
*J'ai trébuché*

## true    vrai

1. A dog is an animal.
   *Le chien est un animal.*

   This is **true**.
   *Ceci est **vrai***

2. Mother read a fairy tale to us.
   *Maman nous a lu un conte de fées.*

   The fairy tale was not **true**.
   *Le conte de fées n'était pas **vrai**.*

## to try    essayer

**Try** to thread the needle.
***Essayez** d'enfiler l'aiguille.*

I try
*J'essaie*

I shall try
*J'essaierai*

I tried
*J'ai essayé*

## tub
## baquet

wash tub
*baquet*
*à lessive*

bath tub
*baignoire*

We often put water in **tubs**.
*Nous mettons souvent de l'eau dans des **baquets**.*

## turn    tour
## to turn    tourner

1. My **turn** is after yours.
   *Mon **tour** vient après le vôtre.*
2. The car **turned** the corner.
   *La voiture a **tourné** le coin.*

I turn
*Je tourne*

I shall turn
*Je tournerai*

I turned
*J'ai tourné*

## twin    jumeau

Tom and Tim are **twins**.
*Tom et Tim sont **jumeaux**.*

They look alike.
*Ils se ressemblent.*

**two**
*deux*

2

Two is a number.
*Deux est un nombre.*
Here are **two** elephants.
*Voici **deux** éléphants.*

**typewriter**
*machine à écrire*

We write with a **typewriter**.
*Nous écrivons avec une **machine à écrire**.*

# U u

Twenty-first letter of the alphabet.
*Vingt-et-unième lettre de l'alphabet.*

**umbrella**
*parapluie*

An **umbrella** keeps off the rain.
*Le **parapluie** protège de la pluie.*

**under**
**sous, en dessous de**

1. The boat goes **under** the bridge.
   *Le bateau passe **sous** le pont.*
2. The ball is **under** the table.
   *La balle est **en dessous de** la table.*

**to understand**
*comprendre*

Do you **understand** your lessons?
***Comprenez**-vous vos leçons ?*

| I understand | I shall understand | I understood |
|---|---|---|
| *Je comprends* | *Je comprendrai* | *J'ai compris* |

**until**  *jusqu'à, jusqu'à ce que*

1. **Until** lunchtime.
   *Jusqu'à l'heure du déjeuner.*
2. We must stay in **until** the rain stops.
   *Nous devons rester à l'intérieur **jusqu'à ce que** la pluie s'arrête.*

**upon**  *sur*

Bill puts one block **upon** another.
*Bill met un cube **sur** l'autre.*

**use**  *usage, emploi*
**to use**  *employer*

1. A knife has a **use**.
   *Un couteau a un **usage**.*
2. It is **used** for cutting.
   *Il est **employé** pour couper.*
   It is useful for cutting.
   *Il est utile pour couper.*
3. Instructions for the **use** of the medicine are written on the label.
   *Les indications concernant l'**emploi** du médicament sont écrites sur l'étiquette.*

| I use | I shall use | I used |
|---|---|---|
| *J'emploie* | *J'emploierai* | *J'ai employé* |

# V v

Twenty-second letter of the alphabet.
*Vingt-deuxième lettre de l'alphabet.*

**vase**  *vase*

Mary puts some flowers in a **vase**.
*Marie met des fleurs dans un **vase**.*

**vegetable**  *légume*

We grow **vegetables** for food.
*Nous faisons pousser des **légumes** pour nous nourrir.*

These are **vegetables**.
*Voici des **légumes**.*

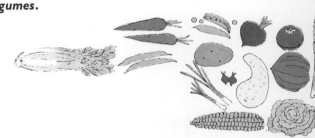

# vehicle   *véhicule*

Some **vehicles** carry people.
*Certains véhicules transportent les gens.*

Other **vehicles** carry goods.
*D'autres véhicules transportent les marchandises.*

These are **vehicles**.
*Voici des véhicules.*

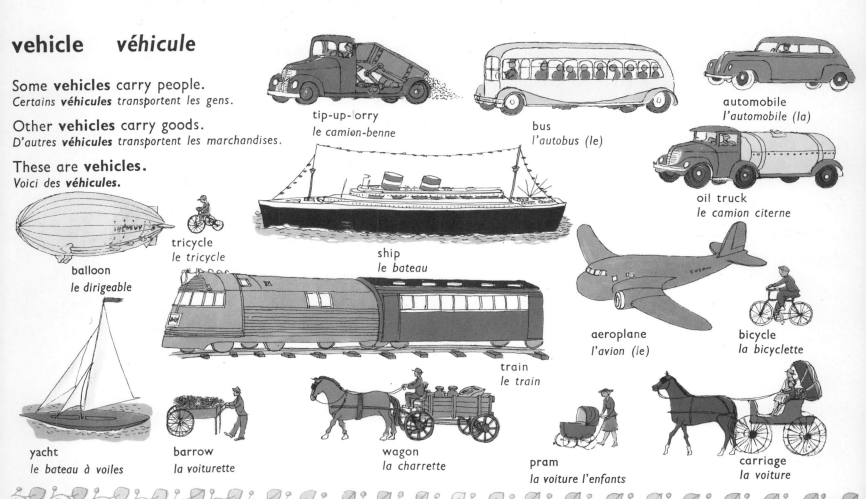

tip-up-orry
*le camion-benne*

bus
*l'autobus (le)*

automobile
*l'automobile (la)*

oil truck
*le camion citerne*

balloon
*le dirigeable*

tricycle
*le tricycle*

ship
*le bateau*

aeroplane
*l'avion (le)*

bicycle
*la bicyclette*

train
*le train*

yacht
*le bateau à voiles*

barrow
*la voiturette*

wagon
*la charrette*

pram
*la voiture l'enfants*

carriage
*la voiture*

---

## very   *très*

The mouse is **very** small.
*La souris est très petite.*

## view   *vue*

We have a **view** from the window.
*Nous avons une vue de la fenêtre.*

## village
## *village*

There are only a few houses in a
**village**.
*Il y a seulement quelques maisons dans un
village.*

## vine
## *vigne, vigne vierge*

A **vine** is a climbing plant.
*La vigne vierge est une plante grimpante.*

## violet
## *violette, violet*

1. A **violet** is a flower.
   *La violette est une fleur.*

2. **Violet** is also a colour.
   *Le violet est aussi une couleur.*

## violin   *violon*

A **violin** makes sweet music.
*Le violon produit une agréable musique.*

## to visit
## *rendre visite, visiter*

1. Ann went **to visit** Betty.
   *Anne alla rendre visite à Betty.*

2. Have you **visited** France?
   *Avez-vous visité la France?*

| I visit | I shall visit | I visited |
|---------|---------------|-----------|
| *Je rends visite* | *Je rendrai visite* | *J'ai rendu visite* |
| *Je visite* | *Je visiterai* | *J'ai visité* |

## voice   *voix*

I speak with my **voice**.
*Je parle avec ma voix.*

I sing with my **voice**.
*Je chante avec ma voix.*

91

# W w

Twenty-third letter of the alphabet.
*Vingt-troisième lettre de l'alphabet.*

## wagon
## camion,
## charrette

1. The toy **wagon** is red.
   *Le **camion**-jouet est rouge.*
2. The **wagon** is full of hay.
   *La **charrette** est pleine de foin.*

## waist    *taille*

Sue has a red belt around her **waist**.
*Suzanne a une ceinture rouge autour de la **taille**.*

## to wait    *attendre*

Bill **is waiting** for the postman.
*Bill **attend** le facteur.*

| I wait | I shall wait | I waited |
|---|---|---|
| *J'attends* | *J'attendrai* | *J'ai attendu* |

## to walk    *marcher*

Peter **walks** to school.
*Pierre **marche** vers l'école.*

Our legs are for **walking**.
*Nos jambes servent à **marcher**.*

| I walk | I shall walk | I walked |
|---|---|---|
| *Je marche* | *Je marcherai* | *J'ai marché* |

## wall    *mur*

Our house has four **walls**.
*Notre maison a quatre **murs**.*

There is a window in one **wall** of my room.
*Ii y a une fenêtre dans un **mur** de ma chambre.*

## to want    *vouloir*

Do you **want** a book?
***Voulez**-vous un livre ?*

| I want | I shall want | I wanted |
|---|---|---|
| *Je veux* | *Je voudrai* | *J'ai voulu* |

## war    *guerre*

When countries are at **war** they are fighting each other.
*Quand les pays sont en **guerre** ils combattent les uns contre les autres.*

## warm    *chaud*
## to warm    *réchauffer*

We wash with **warm** water.
*Nous nous lavons avec de l'eau **chaude**.*

Bob **warms** his hands by the fire.
*Bob **réchauffe** ses mains près du feu.*

| I warm | I shall warm | I warmed |
|---|---|---|
| *Je réchauffe* | *Je réchaufferai* | *J'ai réchauffé* |

## waste    *déchets*
## to waste    *gâcher*

**Waste** paper goes into the wastepaper basket.
*Les vieux papiers (**déchets**) vont dans la corbeille à papiers.*
We **waste** things when we do not use them well.
*Nous **gâchons** les choses quand nous ne les employons pas bien.*

| I waste | I shall waste | I wasted |
|---|---|---|
| *Je gâche* | *Je gâcherai* | *J'ai gâché* |

## watch    *montre*
## to watch    *observer*

1. A **watch** tells time.
   *Une **montre** indique l'heure.*
2. I **watched** the children play.
   *J'**observais** les enfants qui jouaient.*

| I watch | I shall watch | I watched |
|---|---|---|
| *J'observe* | *J'observerai* | *J'ai observé* |

## water    *eau*

**Water** is a liquid.
*L'**eau** est un liquide.*

It has no colour, smell, or taste.
*Elle n'a ni couleur, ni odeur, ni goût.*
**Water** is good to drink.
*L'**eau** est agréable à boire.*

## wave    *vague, ondulation*

1. There are **waves** on the sea.
   *Il y a des **vagues** sur la mer.*
2. Ruth has **waves** in her hair.
   *Ruth a des **ondulations** dans les cheveux.*

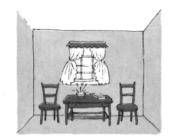

## way
### chemin, manière, façon

1. It is a long **way** home.
   *Il y a un long **chemin** jusqu'à la maison.*

2. This is the **way** to sew.
   *Voici la **manière** dont on coud.*

3. It is a good **way** of keeping busy.
   *C'est une bonne **façon** de s'occuper.*

## we    nous

**We** are two children.
*Nous sommes deux enfants.*

Our names are Ann and Jim.
*Nos noms sont Anne et Jim.*

**We** go to school alone.
*Nous allons tout seuls à l'école.*

Will you give us a ride?
*Voulez-vous nous offrir une promenade en voiture ?*

| we | us | our | ours |
|------|------|------------|-------------------|
| nous | nous | notre, nos | le nôtre, les nôtres |

## to wear
### porter

Betty **is wearing** a new dress.
*Betty **porte** une nouvelle robe.*

| I wear | I shall wear | I wore |
|---------|---------------|-----------|
| Je porte | Je porterai | J'ai porté |

## weather    temps

Sunshine makes clear **weather**.
*Le soleil rend le **temps** clair.*

Rain makes wet **weather**.
*La pluie rend le **temps** humide.*

## week
### semaine

There are seven days in a **week**.
*Il y a sept jours dans une **semaine**.*

A **week** is a measure of time.
*La **semaine** est une mesure du temps.*

## to weigh    peser

Jane **weighs** herself on the scale.
*Jane se **pèse** sur la balance.*

Her **weight** is 52 pounds.
*Son **poids** est de 52 livres.*

| I weigh | I shall weigh | I weighed |
|----------|----------------|-------------|
| Je pèse | Je pèserai | J'ai pesé |

## well    bien

John says he is very **well**.
*Jean dit qu'il va très **bien**.*

He did his work **well**.
*Il a **bien** fait son travail.*

## well    puits

He drew water from the **well**.
*Il a tiré de l'eau du **puits**.*

## west    ouest

**West** is a direction.
*L'**ouest** est une direction.*

The sun goes down in the **west**.
*Le soleil se couche à l'**ouest**.*

## wet
### mouillé, humide

1. The **wet** dog has been in the water.
   *Le chien **mouillé** a été dans l'eau.*

2. The weather is **wet**.
   *Le temps est **humide**.*

## what    quoi, que

1. Of **what** are you thinking?
   *A **quoi** pensez-vous ?*

2. **What** is it?
   *Qu'est-ce que c'est ?*

## wheat    blé

Wheat is a cereal.
*Le **blé** est une céréale.*

We make bread from **wheat**.
*Nous faisons le pain avec du **blé**.*

## wheel    roue

**Wheels** are round.
*Les **roues** sont rondes.*

Cars and trains run on **wheels**.
*Les voitures et les trains roulent sur des **roues**.*

## when    quand

**When** will the clock strike six?
*Quand la pendule sonnera-t-elle six heures ?*

We travel **when** we are on holiday.
*Nous voyageons **quand** nous sommes en vacances.*

# where   où

**Where** is my hat?
*Où est mon chapeau?*

It is on your head!
*Il est sur votre tête.*

# which   *lequel, que*

1. **Which** is the chocolate cake?

   *Lequel est le gâteau au chocolat?*

   The brown one is chocolate.
   *Le brun est le gâteau au chocolat.*
2. It is the one **which** I prefer.
   *C'est celui que je préfère.*

# while
## pendant que

We whistle **while** we work.
*Nous sifflons pendant que nous travaillons.*

# to whisper
## murmurer

Sue **whispers** in Mother's ear.
*Suzon murmure dans l'oreille de maman.*

| I whisper | I shall whisper | I whispered |
|---|---|---|
| *Je murmure* | *Je murmurerai* | *J'ai murmuré* |

# to whistle
## siffler

Bob **whistles** as he walks along.
*Bob siffle pendant qu'il se promène.*

| I whistle | I shall whistle | I whistled |
|---|---|---|
| *Je siffle* | *Je sifflerai* | *J'ai sifflé* |

# white
## blanc

**White** is a colour.
*Le blanc est une couleur.*
Snow is **white.**
*La neige est blanche.*

# who   *qui*

**Who** is at the door?
*Qui est à la porte?*

Is it Father?
*Est-ce papa?*

Father has three children **who** love him.
*Papa a trois enfants qui l'aiment.*

# whole   *entier*

I dropped the cup but it is still **whole**.
*J'ai fait tomber la tasse mais elle est encore entière.*

George ate the **whole** apple.
*Georges a mangé la pomme entière.*

# whom   *que*

The man **whom** we saw in the city.
*L'homme que nous avons vu en ville.*

# whose   *dont*

The boy **whose** dog is white.
*Le garçon dont le chien est blanc.*

# why   *pourquoi*

**Why** do you want your dinner?
*Pourquoi voulez-vous votre dîner?*

Because I am hungry.
*Parce que j'ai faim.*

# wide   *large*

The brook is **wide**.
*Le ruisseau est large.*

# wild   *sauvage*

**Wild** flowers grow in the woods and fields.
*Les fleurs sauvages poussent dans les bois et les champs.*

**Wild** animals do not live near towns
*Les animaux sauvages ne vivent pas près des villes.*

# wind   *vent*

The **wind** blows in the trees.
*Le vent souffle dans les arbres.*

It is a **windy** day today.
*Il fait du vent aujourd'hui.*

94

## to wind    enrouler

Bob **winds** the string around his finger.
*Bob **enroule** la ficelle autour de son doigt.*

I **wind** it around my finger, too.
*Je l'**enroule** aussi autour de mon doigt.*

| I wind | I shall wind | I wound |
|---|---|---|
| J'enroule | J'enroulerai | J'ai enroulé |

## window    fenêtre

A **window** lets in the light.
*La **fenêtre** laisse entrer la lumière.*

**Windows** are made of glass.
*Les **fenêtres** sont en verre.*

## wing    aile

Birds fly with two **wings.**
*Les oiseaux volent avec deux **ailes.***

The plane has red **wings.**
*L'avion a des **ailes** rouges.*

## winter    hiver

**Winter** is the coldest season of the year.
*L'**hiver** est la saison la plus froide de l'année.*

## to wipe    essuyer

Ann **wipes** her hands.
*Anne s'**essuie** les mains.*

| I wipe | I shall wipe | I wiped |
|---|---|---|
| J'essuie | J'essuierai | J'ai essuyé |

## wire    fil (métallique)

Here are some kinds of **wire.**
*Voici plusieurs sortes de **fil** métallique.*

## wish    souhait, vœu
## to wish    désirer

1. You may make a **wish.**
   *Vous pouvez faire un **souhait.***

2. At New Year, we send best **wishes** to our friends.
   *A l'occasion du Nouvel An, nous adressons nos meilleurs **vœux** à nos amis.*

3. I **wish** I were a fireman.
   *Je **désirerais** être un pompier.*

| I wish | I shall wish | I wished |
|---|---|---|
| Je désire | Je désirerai | J'ai désiré |

## witch    sorcière

A **witch** is a bad fairy.
*Une **sorcière** est une mauvaise fée.*

## with    avec

Rover went **with** Bob.
*Rover est parti **avec** Bob.*

## without    sans

Bob came home **without** Rover.
*Bob est rentré à la maison **sans** Rover.*

## wolf    loup

A **wolf** is a wild animal.
*Le **loup** est un animal sauvage.*

## woman    femme

My mother is a **woman.**
*Ma mère est une **femme.***

These are **women.**
*Voici des **femmes.***

## wood    bois

Trees give us **wood.**
*Les arbres nous donnent du **bois.***

Trees grow in the **woods.**
*Les arbres poussent dans les **bois.***

## wool    laine

A sheep has a coat of **wool.**
*Le mouton a une fourrure en **laine.***

We make cloth from **wool.**
*Nous faisons de l'étoffe avec la **laine.***

## word    mot

Every **word** means something.
*Chaque **mot** veut dire quelque chose.*

These are **words**.
*Voici des **mots**.*

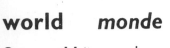

man *homme*  good *bon*  funny *drôle*
jump *sauter*  cat *chat*  doll *poupée*
Mary *Marie*  word *mot*

## work    travail
## to work    travailler

1. Everyone has **work** to do.
   *Chacun a un **travail** à faire.*

2. I **work** at my lessons.
   *Je **travaille** à mes leçons.*

   Father **works** in the city.
   *Papa **travaille** en ville.*

   Mother **works** at home.
   *Maman **travaille** à la maison.*

| I work | I shall work | I worked |
|--------|--------------|----------|
| *Je travaille* | *Je travaillerai* | *J'ai travaillé* |

## world    monde

Our **world** is round.
*Notre **monde** est rond.*

It is called the Earth.
*Il est appelé: la Terre.*

## to wrap    envelopper

Susan **is wrapping** her book.
*Suzanne **enveloppe** son livre.*

| I wrap | I shall wrap | I wrapped |
|--------|--------------|-----------|
| *J'enveloppe* | *J'envelopperai* | *J'ai enveloppé* |

## to write    écrire

Peter **writes** on the blackboard.
*Pierre **écrit** sur le tableau noir.*

| I write | I shall write | I wrote |
|---------|---------------|---------|
| *J'écris* | *J'écrirai* | *J'ai écrit* |

## wrong

## mauvais, mal

1. Sam has his foot in the **wrong** shoe.
   *Sam a son pied dans le **mauvais** soulier.*

   The dog chewed Father's shoe.
   *Le chien a mâché le soulier de papa.*

2. The dog did **wrong**.
   *Le chien a **mal** fait.*

# X x

Twenty-fourth letter of the alphabet.
*Vingt-quatrième lettre de l'alphabet.*

## Xmas    Noël

**Xmas** is a short way of writing Christmas in English.
*"Xmas" est une façon abrégée d'écrire "Noël" en anglais.*

## X-ray    rayons-X

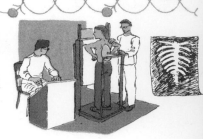

An **X-ray** serves for seeing through solid things.
*Les **rayons-X** servent à voir à travers les objets solides.*

## xylophone    xylophone

I play music on the **xylophone** with little hammers.
*Je fais de la musique sur le **xylophone** avec de petits marteaux.*

# Y y

Twenty-fifth letter of the alphabet.
*Vingt-cinquième lettre de l'alphabet.*

## yarn    laine à tricoter

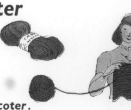

Mother knits with **yarn**.
*Maman tricote avec de la **laine à tricoter**.*

## to yawn  *bâiller*

We **yawn** when we are sleepy.
*Nous **bâillons** quand nous avons sommeil.*

| I yawn | I shall yawn | I yawned |
|---|---|---|
| *Je bâille* | *Je bâillerai* | *J'ai bâillé* |

## year  *année, an*

1. There are twelve months in a **year**.
   *Il y a douze mois dans une **année**.*
2. Pete is twelve **years** old.
   *Pierrot a douze **ans**.*

## yellow  *jaune*

**Yellow** is a colour.
*Le **jaune** est une couleur.*

## yes  *oui*

Is it raining?
*Pleut-il?*

**Yes**, it is raining.
*Oui, il pleut.*

## yesterday  *hier*

**Yesterday** was the day before today.
***Hier** était le jour avant aujourd'hui.*

# Z z

Twenty-sixth letter of the alphabet.
*Vingt-sixième lettre de l'alphabet.*

## zebra  *zèbre*

A **zebra** is a striped animal.
*Un **zèbre** est un animal rayé.*

## zero  *zéro*

**Zero** is a number.
***Zéro** est un nombre.*

**Zero** means none at all.
***Zéro** veut dire: "rien du tout"*

## yet  *déjà*

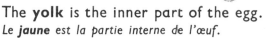

Have the eggs hatched **yet**?
*Les œufs sont-ils **déjà** éclos?*

## yolk  *jaune d'œuf*

The **yolk** is the inner part of the egg.
*Le **jaune** est la partie interne de l'œuf.*

## you  *vous*

**You** are reading this book.
***Vous** êtes en train de lire ce livre.*

What is your name?
*Quel est votre nom?*

| you | your | yours |
|---|---|---|
| *vous* | *votre, vos* | *le vôtre, les vôtres* |

## young  *jeune*

Bruce is **young**.
*Bruce est **jeune**.*

He is only two years old.
*Il a seulement deux ans.*

## zig-zag  *zig-zag*

The red line is **zig-zag**.
*La ligne rouge est en **zig-zag**.*

## zoo  *jardin zoologique*

Father took us to the **zoo**.
*Papa nous a emmenés au **jardin zoologique**.*

# HOW TO SAY THE WORDS

It is not at all easy for us to say French words. We must ask someone who speaks French to help us. Here are some general rules.

## Vowels

| | |
|---|---|
| A | is rather like the A in **ask** (pas, chat). |
| E | is rather like the E in **begin,** (le, je). Push lips forward. |
| | If it is the last letter of a word that has another vowel in it, it is not said at all (plume, poche). |

É, È, and Ê are like A in **ate** (bébé) and E in **bed** (chèvre) and E in **end** (fenêtre).

I and Y are like the EE in **meet** (ami, ici, pyjama).

| | |
|---|---|
| O | is like the O in **bone** (dos, mot). |
| U | is not like any English vowel. Push your lips out to whistle and say "EE." (tu, du). |
| AU | is like the O in **piano** (au, aussi). |
| EU | is like the English **err** (fleur, beurre). |
| OU | is like the U and the OO in **cuckoo** (où, bijou). |

## Consonants

The letters B D F K L M N P R S V are said as in English and H in French is always soft (as in honour).

| | |
|---|---|
| C | is a hard sound, as in **cat**, before another consonant (boucle) and before an A (cabane), an O (col) or a U (cube). |
| C | is soft, as in **face**, before an E (ce) or an I (ciel). |
| G | is a hard sound, as in **gate** before another consonant (grand) and before an A (gare), an O (gomme) or a U (guide). |
| G | is soft as the S in **pleasure** before an E (genou) or an I (bougie). |
| J | is also like the S in **pleasure** (jardin, joli). |
| Q | is always followed by a U (except in the word **coq**). The two together are said like K (qui, quatre). |
| T | is usually as in English, but it is like an S before ION (direction). |
| W | is like a V (wagon). |
| X | is sometimes like the S in **cease** (dix, six). |

Often, when a consonant comes after a vowel right at the end of a word, it is not said at all (rat, drap, pas).